KU-065-815

AGENTS
OF CHANGE

AGENTS OF CHANGE

The Development and Practice of Management Consultancy

Patricia Tisdall

Published in association with the
INSTITUTE OF MANAGEMENT CONSULTANTS

HEINEMANN : LONDON

William Heinemann Ltd
10 Upper Grosvenor Street
London W1X 9PA
LONDON MELBOURNE TORONTO
JOHANNESBURG AUCKLAND

© Institute of Management Consultants 1982
First published 1982
SBN 434 91961 6

Photoset by Deltatype, Ellesmere Port
Printed by Redwood Burn Limited, Trowbridge, Wiltshire

To My Mother

Contents

Preface

I was delighted when the Institute of Management Consultants invited me to write a history of the profession to commemorate its twentieth anniversary. It gave me a chance to find out more about a group of people whose company I have always enjoyed and who have contributed greatly to my personal understanding of how business works. Management consultants often have a talent, knack, skill, flair, call it what you will, of adjusting the pieces of a mental jigsaw into an order which creates a clear picture.

In a sense this book is an attempt to repay that debt in that the aim behind it is to try to improve general understanding of contemporary management consulting, not least by management consultants themselves. I happen to believe that the profession has a valuable contribution to make to industrial society. But I also think that this contribution will only be fully realized if management consultants themselves value the work they do.

I was also, frankly, curious to discover the reality behind the exotic legends which had built up about management consultants and which, within a decade, had mysteriously evaporated. What substance was there behind the gilded, and rather lordly, figures who flitted through the corridors of power when I and my generation first started work in the 1960s?

This book is an attempt to trace the path of British management consultants across almost eight decades of industrial history. It has not been an easy task, not least because British management consultants, unlike some of their American counterparts, are careful not to leave any footprints and are discreet to the point of fanaticism about their clients' affairs. Yet, if management consultancy is a science, and not – as some leading practitioners claim – an art, then it is an applied one. The only way of describing the many variables which influence the end results of the changes arising from a management consultant's activities seemed to be by illustrations from real assignments. From these, others more knowledgeable, and wiser than I, may be able to add to my tentative conclusions from their own experience. I hope I will be forgiven if I seem to have made some arbitrary choices.

I found that the history of management consulting fell into three distinct phases. The first concerned individuals who felt they had a gospel tempered by practical experience of business, which they wanted to spread to others. The second concerned the development of management consulting itself (although in some instances halfheartedly) into a commercial activity in its own right. Although the leaders of the big consultancy practices whose willing gift of time and patience I greatly appreciate, might not agree, I regard the third and current phase, of the return of the individual, as healthy both for the profession and for the millions of people who are directly or indirectly affected by the changes introduced by consultants.

As far as possible, the book has concentrated on people and personalities. This is not only in the interests of readability which is the first duty of the professional writer but again is an attempt to provide information to enable others to add to what I have said from their own knowledge. I am sorry if I have given any offence or embarrassment in the attempt. I agree with those who maintain that management consultancy is a personalized activity which is best carried out by individuals acting as individuals: that it is a matter of human chemistry and warmblooded contact. The intention is not in any way to disparage the contribution of the specialists and scientists who form the business foundation for modern consultancies. It simply seemed that there were other authors who were better equipped to evaluate and explain the much needed work that they do.

This book sets out to give an objective account of the development of management consulting. What the months of painstaking research which lie behind it point to is that one of the profession's most identifiable contributions has been to the development of management itself. It is easy to forget that it is only within the last thirty years that the management function has been separated from that of ownership in Europe.

It is also easy to forget that, while technological changes seem to be taking place almost daily, people's attitudes change much more slowly. It was a salutary experience to go back over the writings and speeches made in the late 1940s by pioneers of the management movement like Stafford Cripps and Lyndall Urwick and to find that so many of the commonsense improvements recommended and accepted then have still to be carried out.

The other most clearly identifiable landmark of management consultancy is in industrial relations in manufacturing industry and the nationalized industries. Most of the framework for incentive, productivity and other payment by results schemes was formed by the early work measurement practitioners. Many of them have turned out badly – because they were allowed to decay, because they were implemented without comprehension or regard for long term consequences, or because they were badly designed in the first place. But it would be a great pity if the advantages of objective measurement of performance were lost in self-recrimination about a stage in an evolutionary process.

I have sidestepped many issues which I know to be of importance to the profession as well as fascinating in their own right. One of these is the definition of a profession and whether management consultancy is a business or a profession. I have also not dealt in any detail with the very great contribution British management consultancy has made overseas both in exporting its own services and in developing new markets for its clients. This is because, it seems to me, business itself transcends national boundaries and that it was to be expected that management consultants too should operate transnationally.

What follows, the author earnestly hopes, is a narrative which, while necessarily selective in the events and personalities described, will contribute to understanding at a turbulent time when not just management consultants but management itself is just beginning to reach maturity. I am very deeply indebted to the many people who have given help and encouragement along the way. In particular, my thanks go to my two mentors, Peter Farr, partner of O. W. Roskill Industrial Consultants, and Len Weaver, the managing director of The P–E Consulting Group. They both care passionately about their profession and have themselves put a great deal of hard work into its future but they did not seek to impose their own views on the author in any way.

My thanks also go to the many people ranging from the past and present leaders of consultancy firms to office workers and clerical staff who entrusted their views to me in interviews. I should like to make a collective acknowledgement to the hundred or so consultants who volunteered case histories and material for use in the book and who are too numerous to mention individually.

I should in addition like to record my very sincere appreciation of the help given by Alex Morley-Smith, the General Secretary of the Institute of Management Consultants, and his two hard-working assistants not only for providing administrative support and allowing me to comb freely through their archives, but also for inspiration and morale boosting during blizzards and train strikes.

A separate paragraph of praise must be devoted to the excellent archivists, whose painstaking research and maintenance of historic papers is too often taken for granted and deserves wider recognition. In particular I would like to thank Gillian Dare, the Librarian of the British Institute of Management; Julia Hallé, Information Scientist at The P–E Consulting Group, and Stuart Dunkeld, Head of International Information at PA Management Consultants, who not only opened their libraries to me but also guided me through them.

PATRICIA TISDALL
April 1982

1
Introducing Management Consultancy

Management consulting is one of those occupations whose influence is disproportionately greater than the numbers engaged in it. Its services are used not only by commercial organizations but by whole governments. Assignments can range in scale from planning a nation's health service to rearranging the layout of a warehouse.

At one time it seemed as though consultants were everywhere and their influence boundless. They appeared an intellectual elite whose reputation for ruthlessly eliminating waste and bureaucracy was wooed by every conceivable type of organization. The very announcement that management consultants had been called in was sufficient to send ripples of fear along the corridors of the most august of institutions.

In fact, the increase in consultants has been nothing like as great as was predicted in their heyday during the 1960s when, according to one estimate, the total could be as high as 8,000 by 1980. Instead, the number of management consultants practising in Britain appears to have stabilized in the last decade at about 5,000. Nor has the way the industry is structured followed the expected path. In terms of market share, the original big independent practices have collectively given way, on the one hand to accountants' subsidiaries, and on the other to large numbers of small firms and self-employed sole practitioners. From being highly concentrated on a few activities under a handful of trading names, management consultancy has splintered into dozens of specialist sub-categories.

Structural change
One of the effects of fragmentation has been to focus responsibility

for professional integrity on individuals rather than their employing organizations. This trend has been mirrored in the membership growth and development of the Institute of Management Consultants and a relative decline in support from the Management Consultants Association, which represents firms.

Externally, the fragmentation in structure has made management consultants both more approachable and less glamorous. There is more emphasis on implementation – a feature which British consultants have consistently stressed – and less on theoretical concepts. Consultants are working alongside managements which in turn have become better educated, more articulate, and are highly conscious of obtaining value for their money. A new generation of consultants, who are also entrepreneurial businessmen in their own right, has grown up; and they are looking at new methods of harnessing their colleagues' talents to those of their clients.

Although the environment in which consultants operate has altered radically, the basic elements of their profession remain the same. While his assignment may deal only in a specific area, the management consultant always aims to take account of its application to the total context. This is seen as the fundamental difference between a straightforward specialist and a management consultant. In explaining this characteristic, Geoffrey Buss, the 1981–82 president of the Institute of Management Consultants, uses a metaphorical letter 'T' in which the cross bar represents the generalist and the vertical stroke the specialist skills. The change as he perceives it since he entered consultancy in the 1950s is that the vertical line was about a quarter of the depth it is now. 'There is an increasing need for the vertical line representing specialisation to be ever deeper but that mustn't overshadow the fact that there is a minimum breadth that you need right across the range,' he says.

Len Weaver, managing director of the P–E Consulting Group, expresses it differently:

> Much of the skill which has come into consultancy today is recognising that each client company is absolutely unique in terms of its past history, its origins and evolution. Its history of industrial relations, its management style and its cultural attitudes. It is also unique in its working attitudes – what people feel is expected from them as a normal day's work, not only from the shop floor, but also from the

staff – the salesmen and the managers. You have got to understand why it is unique. You have got to understand what makes that company tick before you attempt to make it tick any faster. If you don't you will break the mainspring . . . the art of consulting is achieving successful change even though it may not be as much change as the purist would like.

Art or science?

The development of management consultancy parallels that of professional management. Just as in management, there is a dichotomy between approaches which are based on formal axioms and those which depend largely on intuition. Consultants, like managers, have found that precise observation, measurement, and experimentation need to be combined with communication and persuasion to produce best results.

'Change agents' is the phrase most often used by management consultants themselves to describe what they do because their services are most in demand whenever changes are contemplated. Traditionally their assistance falls into three broad categories: as experts; as extra pairs of hands; and as facilitators or catalysts. Consultants rarely initiate the changes – the responsibility for this must lie with their client organizations. However, their impartial status and fresh viewpoint often enable them to suggest new answers to old problems. They can also be used to check and endorse unpopular decisions – and all too frequently carry the blame for them afterwards. Increasingly they are being employed to give practical temporary assistance.

The definitions used by the Institute of Management Consultants trip less easily off the tongue but are more comprehensive. They read as follows:

Management Consulting. The service provided by an independent and qualified person or persons in identifying and investigating problems concerned with policy, organization procedures and methods, recommending appropriate action and helping to implement these recommendations.

Management Consultants. Persons whose principal activity is in the independent practice of management consulting, who arrive at their recommendations by factual investigation and with due regard to the need for preserving perspective. They have adequate experience in providing such advice in at least one of the fields of activity required by the Institute.

In 1976 the Council agreed that the term Independent Practice 'shall include consultants engaged as "in house" consultants who meet the required standards of knowledge, experience and competence and are free at all times to offer objective and independent advice'.

According to the Institute's notes of guidance assignments are likely to incorporate one or more of the following four requirements: independent and impartial advice on an issue or policy; extra executive manpower in the analysis and solution of identified problems, assistance in the implementation of a specific project, i.e. where the need is urgent but the existing executive staff cannot be expected to devote sufficient time to it; and, innovation and the forward look.

Practical assistance

Although he considers temporary management to be a growing area Brian Woodhead, the 1982–83 President of the Institute and proprietor of his own company, expresses some reservations on this score:

> Finding himself in the hot seat with executive authority as temporary works manager or personnel director or whatever is not always what a management consultant is good at . . . Sometimes consultants can do it and are right for it. But we [his own company] would differentiate between consultancy and temporary management by saying that consultancy work is generally when you are changing things. Temporary management is when you are running them as they are, where the main thing is to keep the day to day business running along established lines . . . I don't think it's fair for a manager who is doing his job and running his department to be expected to give his attention to designing and implementing a major change.

Trends for the future

Mobility both in the geographical sense and in the ability to switch between projects is an important distinction between the consultant and the manager. Apart from an instinctive liking for variety, consultants tend not to be good at taking decisions – they are trained to weigh up all points of view rather than to opt for a single course of action and stick to it. With a few distinguished exceptions, there has traditionally been little interchange between managers and consultants in Britain – unlike the United States, where it is commonplace for an executive to spend a year or so with a management consultancy while he looks round for something else. Greater cross-fertilization of this kind is something which Woodhead, with others, believes will be a trend for the future. For one thing, it removes the sting from one of the most common criticisms clients make: if the consultant is so good at management, why has he not done it?

> At the moment we are doing a very interesting job for a large group which is assessing the scope for a completely new kind of retailing operation in the Do-It-Yourself field. We are lucky to have a chap who grew his own DIY business into a multi million pound organisation and then sold out. He is very wealthy and has his yacht and so on, but he got bored. We have him working alongside one of our directors on this project. He is adding that intuition, that knowledge of the marketplace, and what you can and can't do in a retailing operation to the client's own expertise. The combination is quite powerful.
>
> This is a man who really has done it. He can always answer the accusation of 'Well you are so clever, why haven't you done it.' He can say, as not very many consultants can, 'I have a successful business career in my own right and I can stand on equal terms with you, Mr Client.' A lot of the consultants further down the scale in the big firms are always vulnerable to the accusation that those who can do, and those who can't teach.

In the meantime, the consultant who crosses the bridge into a client organization and vice versa is a rarity in Britain. A survey carried out by the Institute of Management Consultants found that three-quarters of practising consultants definitely intended to remain in consultancy. The three main attractions of the job were cited as variety, worthwhile projects and the development of skills . . . As for the drawbacks of consultancy as a profession there was a clear indication that most respondents considered the primary reason for not remaining a consultant was the amount of time spent away from home.

Problems associated with constant travel allied with a desire to develop a specialist area are among the most frequent reasons given by the many consultants who have opted out of the big firms to set up on their own account.

They may, as some ruefully admit, in fact travel just as much, but at least feel their destinations are under their own control. There is also some evidence of an underlying disillusionment with the way in which their plans were being implemented. The desire to make things better is an important motivator for all consultants who tend to prefer the description 'company doctor' to the hated nickname of 'efficiency expert'. Working in smaller groups they feel that much closer to their clients and therefore able to influence the implementation of their recommendations to a greater extent.

There is no evidence, however, that fragmentation has brought any greater interest in the problems of smaller firms – an aim long cherished by Government. Management Consultants Association statistics, which cover 25 of the big consultancies and are a useful indicator of trends, show that the proportion of work carried out for clients with over 200 employees has, if anything, increased during the last few years. The percentage of larger clients was 63 per cent in 1976 and 72 per cent in 1981 whereas there was a much slighter movement in the proportion employing less than 200 during the same period. This stood at 27 per cent in 1976 and 28 per cent in 1981.

The difficulty of providing a consultancy service to small firms is basically one of economics. This was identified very lucidly by the Bolton Committee on Small Firms which reported in November 1971.

Basically, there are two serious difficulties in providing consultancy for small firms: first, the consultancy is not, as might be thought, necessarily more simple than advising a large firm, but in some ways more difficult: and second, the strong sales-resistance of the typical small businessman necessitates a powerful marketing effort which the majority of consultants, given a high level of demand for their services, are not prepared to make. It is consequently very difficult to run such services profitably.

Because the small firm will rarely have identified correctly the problem giving rise to his need for advice, the consultant will need very wide experience since his first task will often be to survey the whole of the firm's operations and identify the basic trouble. This point was well made by a representative of the Management Consultants Association who said:

'If ICI ask you to come in and do some time study on the loading bay you can be pretty sure that is what they want, whereas if a small business asks you to do that, you have not a clue whether that is really the problem.'

The small businessman who calls in a consultant is normally aware only that something is going wrong and he expects the consultant to diagnose the trouble and suggest a solution. Very often he is a lonely man, unwilling to discuss his problem with his staff and having nobody else with whom to share the decision making. In these circumstances, if the consultant can gain the businessman's confidence he may perform a very valuable service in providing a sympathetic ear, putting the problems in perspective (which involves pointing out that they are not unique, but have probably been faced and solved in most successful business) and generally acting as a trusted counsellor. It is very hard for a young and inexperienced man, however able, to fulfil this role, so for this reason also a more senior man is required. But it takes time to build up such a relationship and the time of such men is expensive. Though it may be possible to expand still more rapidly the total number of consultants, the number of those who meet the small firm's needs will be always limited, and there will always be other calls on their time.

[Report by the Bolton Committee on Small Firms, 1971]

Although the sharp downturn in demand for consultancy services which turned an anticipated 15 or 20 per cent increase into a decline had already taken place by the time the report was published, the Committee's review was mainly carried out during the boom years. Since it was a high level of demand from existing clients as much as consultants' selling costs which hampered consultants in moving into small firms, it would be reasonable to suppose that the lean years might bring a change.

One of the reasons why this has not happened to any great extent is that consultants will, not surprisingly, concentrate their efforts where they are likely to get repeat orders – and this means large organizations with many departments. One of the strongest indications of the value of consultancy work is the loyalty of its users. While there may be strong resistance to the idea initially, once a firm uses a consultant it will tend to come back for more. The experience of one large consultancy practice which is that around 70 per cent of its work comes from existing clients is typical of many.

The problem is in gaining the initial introduction. The Bolton Committee suggested that advertising might be the answer. The conclusion reached by PA Management Consultants, the country's largest consultancy organization which resigned from the Management Consultants Association in order to advertise its services, is that it is not. The cost of the advertisements far outweighed the additional business which resulted.

A tendency towards extrovert salesmanship was a characteristic shared by most of the founders of the profession. Frank Gilbreth's children recall that in the 1920s their father had a knack of setting up publicity pictures which tied in with his motion study projects. 'While he was working for the Remington people, there were the newsreels of us typing touch system on Moby Dick, the white typewriter with the blind keys. Later, when he got a job with an automatic pencil company, he decided to photograph us burying a pile of wooden pencils.' In the 1930s Charles Bedaux advertised his firm in neon lights. Lyndall Urwick promoted the aims of consultancy as well as management by his appearances on public platforms. Both Ernest Butten (founder of PA) and David Nicolson (who joined The P–E Consulting Group in 1946) made cold sales calls on likely prospects.

Sir David remembers visiting the international vice presidents of some 300 to 400 American companies because he felt his company could provide local knowledge about investment projects in Europe. 'In every case I did what every good salesman should do. You get the chap to talk about his troubles. You don't give him a spiel. You get him to do the talking by asking questions like, "What do you find difficult in planning your European expansion programme?". We got a lot of big clients, people like General Foods and so on. But the thing I hadn't reckoned on was, at the end of two or three years of this, I had a postgraduate course in international business operation because every international VP had told me his problems and we discussed how he was tackling it. So it was very educational for me.'

By the 1960s, however, management consultants were becoming wary about publicizing their activities. Modern consultants trace a dislike of full-blooded advertising to the reaction of the Institute of Chartered Accountants against the sales tactics used by a Chicago-based firm, George S. May, in 1961. Despite official professional disapproval, advertising went on, of course, although at a personalized level where, in any case, it is most effective. Methods range from an exchange of business cards on golf course or cocktail party to an uninvited telephone call or letter, office or factory visit. A point which too many of the second generation heads of consultancy practices were reluctant to grasp was that there is a direct relationship between the effectiveness of such methods and the seniority of the person applying them.

Even today, there is a strong tendency to rely on very expensively printed brochures containing no relevant figures and little specific information.

Fragmentation is helping to ensure that sales efforts are more directly related to clients' requirements, but it will be a slow process. The accountancy practices, of course, have the permanent built-in advantage through their audit work not only of a regular supply of work but also of introductions to potential management consultant users. One of the largest of the accounting firms is said to have positioned a management consultant at the end of every corridor of auditors' offices so as to ease communications between the two activities.

Origins and development

The foundations of modern British management consultancy practices have two main trunks: accountancy and work measurement. Work measurement which in turn stems from pioneering individuals like Frederick W. Taylor (1856–1915) and Frank B. Gilbreth (1869–1924) is the older of the two. It was this which formed the basis for consultancy practices such as Inbucon (formed 1926), Urwick, Orr & Partners and The P–E Consulting Group (both formed in 1934) and PA Management Consultants (formed 1943). These four companies accounted for three-quarters of all consultancy work in 1956 when it was estimated that about £4 million annually was being spent on consultancy assignments and there were about 1,000 experienced consultants practising. Today they account for less than half a market estimated at £200 million annually and consisting of about 5,000 consultants. PA the youngest is also by far the largest, with a total group turnover including services other than management consultancy which in 1981 amounted to about £54 million and an estimated 25 per cent share of the consulting work originating in Britain. Next comes Inbucon which turns over around £31 million followed by The P–E Consulting Group with an income of £8.4 million in 1981 and Urwick Orr with about £4 million.

As business became more complex and administration of it grew, so the management consulting subsidiaries formed by the accountancy firms became more dominant with an added boost being given by the introduction of electronic data processing systems and equipment. Today the consulting arms of four large accountancy firms – Coopers Lybrand Associates, Peat Marwick Mitchell, Arthur Anderson and Price Waterhouse – rank among the ten largest providers of management consultancy services.

Early management consultants, who were required to hold a university degree or to be a member of a professional body under the Institute of Management Consultants rules, were mostly engineers and accountants. Gradually, as large companies learned to conduct their own work measurement, demand switched to other areas. Production management shrank from about 40 per cent of the work carried out by firms in membership of the Management Consultants Association in the mid 1960s to less than 20 per cent by early 1980. On the other hand, the statistics show an increase in finance and administration work from about 20 per cent to 30 per cent during the same period.

Out of the two original main trunks have stemmed branches which are as various as business itself. Biggest of these is personnel management and selection representing over 20 per cent of income and taking in the searching for and placing of individual executives in the right jobs as well as training of staff at all grades. At first management consultants expressed considerable reservations about head hunting, unlike their American counterparts, but most now regard it as a naturally complementary service. British consultants constantly stress their willingness to live with their proposals and implement them as one of the main differences between them and their American counterparts some of whom they scornfully describe as the 'recommend and run brigade'.

But Jim Kennedy, the editor and publisher of a newsletter for consultants in the United States, considers that the differences between European management consultants and Americans are largely cosmetic: far outweighed by the similarities.

One of the greatest levellers of national differences has been the spread of consultancy work associated with electronic data processing which, within the last decade, has swept through all sectors of management consultants' operation. Not only did English become the language accepted by the big computer manufacturers led by IBM but the systems stemming from the equipment have been applied internationally. A similar international flavour pervades all the highly specialist areas which have spun off from the micro-electronics revolution.

Computer software has already largely replaced work study as the main plank of consulting incomes, accounting for about a third of the total, and rising. Advanced technology generally and in particular telecommunications and office automation are regarded as continuing to be prime growth areas for the foreseeable future. However, the thirst for advice about the microprocessor was not the only change to hit management consulting in the last five years. The slimming down processes forced on private sector industrial and commercial organizations, which provide over 80 per cent of management consultancy income, boosted large numbers of very bright, professionally trained managers up through the ranks. Suddenly, management consultants were no longer the only experts. In fact, in many cases the expertise they had gained in the pre micro-electronic era was seen to be distinctly rusty.

At the end of the 1960s, when the explosion in demand for specialist expertise occurred, most senior management consultants were chasing organizational corporate development and policy assignments. Since these are the closest to the ultimate decision takers they sit on top of all the other work rather like cream on milk and represent the pinnacle of most consultants' aspirations, but, alas, little more than 10 per cent of fee income.

The combined effect of demand for knowledge about advanced technology and abrupt sharpening up in client management at this time was traumatic. Management consultants' collective ego as well as their incomes took a hard, but probably in the long run healthy, knock. What followed has been an extensive and successful catching up and slimming down exercise. The main question now being asked is whether the specialist pendulum has swung too far.

Lurking on the sidelines waiting only for another economic boom is a potential time bomb in industrial relations. The last headlong dash for high wages regardless of the consequences was only halted by one of the deepest recessions manufacturing industry has ever experienced. If the gains in productivity made during the recession are lost in a similar rush once it is over, then the economic effect could well be disastrous. Sir Raymond Pennock, president of the Confederation of British Industry and chairman of BICC (who incidentally, also describes himself as an industrial historian) asks:

Will our 1981 increase in the ability to compete against exporters and importers through improved output per man and moderate wage settlements be maintained and progress still further? Or will we, in time of up-turn, resume the muscular rituals which have directly led us in a world recession to have six Britons unemployed for every four in France and Germany?

Any discussion of this crucial question is usually dominated by what is happening today, next week or next month. But although this gives urgency to the question, it does not get to the heart of the matter and the heart of the matter is that in many parts of British industry, industrial relations are still nothing like good enough. Whatever the reductions in strike-free days may show, in far too many companies relationships between managers and managed are still based on suspicion and misunderstanding which is in turn based on lack of knowledge of the economic facts which surround their mutual interests.
[*The Times*, 23 March 1982]

Management consultants have a unique contribution to make to industrial relations. Good relationships with trade unions and worker representatives were a fundamental aim of the present generation of large consulting practices and one that they lived up to. They therefore start with a heritage of respect from both sides of a negotiating table. Second, they have a historical body of knowledge in that they inspired most of the early productivity schemes. Third, their impartial status, if correctly applied, can enable them to prevent salt being rubbed into the wounds caused by old grievances.

Given the marketing skills which many consultants have acquired, it takes only a comparatively small adjustment to turn from productivity schemes based on manpower reductions to those linked to the enrichment of existing jobs and the creation of new ones to the benefit of everyone concerned. One of the first effects of the economic upturn will be to reveal shortages of skilled workers in key areas in construction and engineering as well as in sales and personnel management. Consultants will be needed to apply the new programmed learning packages to fill the gaps. Will the recently fragmented management consulting structure cope, particularly if its coffers are depleted by investment in advanced technology?

Or will they be overtaken by a separate job evaluation, training and career counselling service as they were by the employment bureaux and software houses? If employers heed Sir Raymond Pennock's warnings there will be a spate of employee involvement and communications activity. Again, will management consultants rise to the occasion?

The prospects are not good. Although consultancies have identified the people or human sector as an area of future growth, it is seen as one which is far distant and low in priority. Familiarity with the problems is a weakness as well as a strength in that sufficient time has elasped for past mistakes to show up. Management consulting is only just coming of age as a profession. Is it mature enough to go back over old ground and try again?

2
The Pioneers

The origins of modern management consultancy stem from the application of scientific methods to business organization. But its development as an accepted management tool lies as much in the personalities of the early pioneers as in the results they produced. The first management consultants were more than experimental business scientists. They combined a strong dash of opportunism, hunch and some flamboyance with systematic thinking – a disconcerting combination which remains a feature of many management consultants to this day.

Although dividing lines soon became blurred, the early practitioners concentrated mainly on the productive organization of people rather than on machines or finance. This was a new concept when it was first introduced in the United States at the end of the last century. Previously, industrial labour was regarded as plentiful and cheap; and therefore an increase in the output of each individual was considered of little importance. Management consultancy, then called industrial engineering, first gained a toehold against a background of skill shortages and fierce price competition, initially in the United States but later in Britain, after the outbreak of World War I forced output to be stepped up in steel milling, munitions, and shipbuilding.

To reach maturity, management consultancy also required a change in the traditional attitudes of businessmen, and a willingness to delegate responsibility and to seek outside advice. The practice of management consultancy is closely interwoven with the development of management itself, an institution which largely did not exist at the end of the nineteenth century when businesses were directed by the owners or their families. The sharp distinction in status which then existed between the owners of a business and their employees has lingered much longer in Britain than in the United States.

With their independent status, the consultants were able to assist the levelling out process by bridging the gap between the proprietors and the newly emerging professional managers.

The father of scientific management

It is not surprising therefore, that Frederick W. Taylor (1856–1915) whose tomb at Germantown, near Philadelphia carries the inscription 'The Father of Scientific Management' should also be considered one of the first management consultants. Early in his life, Taylor's failing eyesight forced him to exchange an academic career for work in an engineering machine shop. Having served an apprenticeship in several trades he was rapidly promoted until at the early age of 31 he was made chief engineer of the Midvale Steel Works. There he began to try to work out answers to basic industrial questions such as, 'Which is the best way to do a job?' and 'What should constitute a day's work?' He then extended his studies further and endeavoured to establish basic principles of management which would apply to all fields of industrial activity. One of these he later described as 'the division of work into almost equal shares between management and the workers, each department taking over the work for which it is best fitted; instead of the former condition in which almost all of the work and the greater part of the responsibility were thrown on the men! It was these principles, extended and applied, which formed the basis of what has been called 'scientific management'.

One of the characteristics of a good management consultant is that he will question assumptions even if he risks ridicule by doing so. Another is that he will apply logical processes to reaching answers even if the problem concerns something as seemingly trivial as a shovel! When in 1898 Taylor went to the Bethlehem Steel Works, he became interested in the disparity of loads handled by the 600 individual shovellers at the plant. He found, for instance that shovellers were lifting loads of 3½ lbs when handling certain types of coal but up to 38 lbs when moving ore.

Experiments were carried out with different sizes of loads and with shovels of varying weights and designs to discover an optimum load. Eventually, Taylor concluded that a load of 21½ lbs enabled the average man to shovel the maximum tonnage of material in one day. He therefore provided different types of shovels for the different materials, but each was so designed that it could carry a maximum of 21½ lbs.

More significantly in business planning terms, the experiments enabled fairly precise predictions to be made as to the amount of work that would be done in the yard during the ensuing day. On this basis Taylor was able to establish a planning department to carry out the calculations. The standard also enabled each man to be made responsible for his own work and to be paid a bonus for reaching his target instead of working as an unidentified member of a large gang.

These early shovelling experiments were developed into a technique known as 'Time Study'. Each cycle of an operation was broken down into small groups of motions called 'elements'. Each element was timed separately with a stopwatch and the elapsed time of each motion determined. From his time study calculations Taylor was able to show that there were very large and preventable losses of efficiency in most industrial operations which could be recognized and eliminated.

Motion study

The drive for increased efficiency also inspired two other outstanding pioneers of scientific management, Frank B. Gilbreth and his wife Lillian. The example, teaching, and sheer exuberance of the Gilbreths has had a profound effect on the development of management consultancy. Their firm, Gilbreth Inc., was employed to improve efficiency by many major industrial concerns in Britain and Germany as well as the United States between 1910 and 1924. After Frank Gilbreth died in 1924, his wife Lillian carried on lecturing, advising and giving inspiration to generations of management consultants until her own death in 1972.

Like Frederick Taylor, Frank Gilbreth was more than a mere theorist. Born into a New England family of Scottish origin in 1868 and brought up by a widowed ex-schoolteacher mother, Gilbreth exchanged his studies at the Massachusetts Institute of Technology to become a junior apprentice on a building site. One of his early discoveries was the difference in methods used in laying bricks. Gilbreth noted that three distinct sets of movements were used by one craftsman – one set when he was working slowly, another when he was working quickly and a third set when he was demonstrating to a pupil. From these observations he concluded that many of the movements employed were unnecessary and unplanned, and he proceeded by systematic study to develop methods to reduce fatigue and to increase output.

During his first week at work, Gilbreth made so many suggestions about how bricks could be laid faster and better that the foreman threatened repeatedly to fire him. Gilbreth, however, persevered and within a year had designed a scaffold which made him the fastest bricklayer on the site. The principle of the scaffold was that loose bricks and mortar were always at the level of the top of the wall being built. The other bricklayers had to lean over to get their materials. Gilbreth did not. The foreman scoffed, but he had identical scaffolds built for all the men on the job and even suggested that Gilbreth send the original to the Mechanics Institute where it won a prize.

Later, on the foreman's recommendation, Dad was made foreman of a crew of his own. He achieved such astonishing speed records that he was promoted to superintendent, and then went into the contracting business for himself, building bridges, canals, industrial towns and factories. Sometimes, after the contract was finished, he was asked to remain on the job to instal his motion study methods within the factory itself.

By the time he was twenty-seven, he had offices in New York, Boston and London. He had a yacht, smoked cigars and had a reputation as a snappy dresser.

Mother (Lillian Moller) came from a well-to-do family in Oakland, California. She had met Dad in Boston while she was en route to Europe on one of those well-chaperoned tours for fashionable young ladies of the nineties.

Mother was a Phi Beta Kappa and a psychology graduate of the University of California. In those days women who were scholars were viewed with some suspicion. When Mother and Dad were married [in 1904] the Oakland paper said: 'Although a graduate of the University of California, the bride is nonetheless an extremely attractive young woman.' Indeed she was. So it was Mother the psychologist and Dad the motion study man and general contractor, who decided to look into the new field of the psychology of management.

[*Cheaper by the Dozen* by Frank Gilbreth junior and Ernestine Gilbreth Carey. London: William Heinemann, 1949]

Apart from the scaffold, another of Gilbreth's early innovations was a system of controlling building programmes based on forms and records supplemented by daily photographs which helped him to study the details of the methods used in each job. In addition, it gave him up-to-date progress information. During his period as a building contractor he met many of his contemporaries who were interested in more academic studies of management. Included among them was Frederick Taylor.

An inauspicious meeting

Gilbreth's first contact with Taylor was unfortunate. He met a stranger who turned out to be Taylor's assistant using a stopwatch to time bricklayers on one of his sites one morning. The stranger had asked neither the workers nor Gilbreth if he might make the study. An even greater sin in the motion study expert's eyes was that the stranger had also not enquired if the methods which he was so carefully timing were considered to be fully developed.

The incident impressed Gilbreth unfavourably. A large man, tall, weighing over fourteen stone, with red hair and an impulsive temperament, he expressed his objections forcefully. First, in his opinion, it was entirely wrong to take a secret time study; and second, working methods must be checked for accuracy before any records were made. Later, when Taylor suggested that he might care to collaborate in the production of a book on bricklaying, Gilbreth declined, feeling that the difference between their outlooks was too fundamental to be resolved harmoniously.

One reason for the conflict was the marked difference in approaches. Taylor began to develop his interest in management problems when he realized that the limitations of the worker restricted the potential productivity of the machine. Gilbreth, on the other hand, started with the human factor. His own concern for the human element was doubly reinforced by his wife's inclination and training. A comparatively early discovery of the husband and wife partnership was that the best way of getting co-operation out of employees in a factory was to form a joint employer-employee board, which would make work assignments on a basis of personal choice and aptitude. It was also Gilbreth's suggestion that their marriage was to involve partnership in his work as well as partnership in the home.

Fortunately for them both, Mrs Gilbreth remained intensely interested in her husband's work in motion study and in the ideas on management which he had developed in his organization. She encouraged him to put his thoughts on paper, and together they published many articles and treatises, gradually branching out from the building trade into the broader applications of scientific management – as well as bringing up a family of twelve children.

Gilbreth's main disagreement with Taylor was over the use of the stopwatch as the starting point for studies designed to improve working methods. While he admired the older man's courage and analytical ability, Gilbreth maintained it was bad practice to make a time study to set times until the best and most economical method of performing the operation had been established. In addition, he considered that such measurements should be made only with the full consent and co-operation of the worker and that they should not be subject to the error of the observer – as well as bitterly resenting the making of secret time studies of reluctant employees on emotional grounds.

Taylor was interested mainly in the time factor. He approached method and motion as an ancillary task to the practice of his time studies. The Gilbreths, on the other hand, were more interested in devising the most economical methods and the most effective layout of work space, followed by the motion study. They regarded elapsed time as a secondary consideration.

Therbligs

To distinguish their field of research from that of Taylor the Gilbreths coined the term 'motion study'. In 1917 they propounded the first definition of motion study: that it consists of dividing the work into fundamental elements; analysing these elements separately and in relation to one another; and from these studied elements, when timed, building methods of least waste. They also invented the 'Therblig' to describe elemental motions – a term used in work measurement to this day.

> The Therbligs were discovered, or maybe a better word would be diagnosed, by Dad and Mother. Everybody has seventeen of them, they said, and the Therbligs can be used in such a way as to make life difficult or easy for their possessor.
>
> A lazy man, Dad believed, always makes the best use of his Therbligs

because he is too indolent to waste motions. Whenever Dad started to do a new motion study project at a factory, he'd always begin by announcing he wanted to photograph the motions of the laziest man on the job.

'The kind of fellow I want,' he'd say, 'is the fellow who is so lazy he won't even scratch himself. You must have one of those around some place. Every factory has them.'

Dad named the Therbligs for himself. Gilbreth spelled backwards, with a slight variation. They were the basic theorems in his business and resulted indirectly in such things as foot levers to open garbage cans, special chairs for factory workers, redesign of typewriters, and some aspects of the assembly line technique.

Using Therbligs, Dad had shown Regal Shoe Company clerks how they could take a customer's shoe off in seven seconds, and put it back on again and lace it up in twenty-two seconds.

Actually a Therblig is a unit of motion or thought. Suppose a man goes into the bathroom to shave. We'll assume that his face is all lathered and he is ready to pick up his razor. He knows where the razor is, but first he must locate it with his eye. That is 'search', the first Therblig. His eye finds it and comes to rest – that's 'find', the second Therblig. Third comes 'select', the process of sliding the razor prior to the fourth Therblig, 'grasp'. Fifth is 'transport loaded', bringing the razor up to the face, and sixth is 'position', getting the razor set on the face. There are eleven other Therbligs – the last one is 'think'!

When Dad made a motion study, he broke down each operation into a Therblig, and then tried to reduce the time taken to perform each Therblig.

Perhaps certain parts to be assembled could be painted red and others green, so as to reduce the time required for 'search' and 'find'. Perhaps the parts could be moved closer to the object being assembled so as to reduce the time required for 'transport loaded'.

[*Cheaper by the Dozen*, 1949]

Sales consultancy

Dr Harold Whitehead was an early practitioner of a form of management consultancy rather different from the work study principles propounded by the Gilbreths and Frederick Taylor. For one thing he was more concerned with sales and marketing than production. For another he had arrived at his profession via the business school route – a form of entry which was, and still is, much more prevalent in the United States than in Britain.

Whitehead first visited the United States at the age of 26 in order to purchase some window fittings which were required in London.

While he was there, he was asked to speak about the flaws in American salesmanship to a businessmen's association in Hartford, Connecticut. Whitehead, who later remarked, ruefully, that he had a tendency to say 'yes' too often, agreed. This led to requests for similar talks which, eventually, some six years later, in 1912, led to a lectureship at the College of Business Administration of Boston University.

Like other professors at American business colleges of the day, Whitehead was asked for practical as well as theoretical answers to business problems. An early assignment came from a pupil at one of the University's evening courses, a florist. She had a problem in collecting payment for small charge accounts. Whitehead recalled that she asked 'Could you write me a letter to get them to pay up? It would save me a stack of money to get these small accounts paid promptly.' 'Yes' he said (once again) and wrote the following:

Dear Mr X,

Would you mind telling me the kind of letter I should write you which would ensure prompt payment of the enclosed amount and at the same time retain your good will?

Yours, etc.

For this he received $5 – his first fee as a consultant! The letter also proved successful in getting the bills paid.

His second client was a lady who ran a haberdashery shop in Boston. She attended an evening course on Retail Store Management and wanted to know why she could not grow – why she just made a bare living but never got new customers. Whitehead visited the shop and thought it looked drab and unattractive, with no proper window display, just a jumble of toys and oddments. He then arranged to have the window properly dressed by some of his students as an 'exercise'. The inside display was also made attractive and both window and inside displays had 'sales tickets' to attract attention.

The business doubled its turnover following these attentions –but it remained a very tiny business and no fee was charged. Instead, the owner insisted that if Whitehead's wife wanted anything she could have it at cost!

What Whitehead considers to be his first real consultancy job, however, was carried out in 1918. It concerned a family company in Massachusetts which had two factories making popular-priced men's shoes. These were sold through a limited number of wholesalers but sales were dwindling and the business was hardly breaking even.

The owner approached Whitehead because he wanted someone outside the business to tell him the facts, however unpalatable, in order to help him to decide what to do. He invited Whitehead to spend three months to make a study and come up with recommendations. Whitehead recalled:

> Talks with executives were a first step in the investigation, as it was felt wise, as well as necessary, to make them realise that they were the first to be consulted. This is a policy I have always followed and I believe it to be a 'must' in management consultancy.
>
> With an accumulation of information, it was made clear that there were three possible answers to the problem.
> 1. Continue as at present, but concentrate production in one factory. This could ensure a ten-year extension of life, at a guess.
> 2. Advertise a trade name shoe and sell direct to the retailer and also, to make shoes for the big departmental stores and mail-order houses under other brand names.
> 3. Organise a chain store business and eventually drop all other trade outlets. For the time being to accept orders secured with no selling cost from the dwindling wholesale business.
>
> Possibility number one was ruled out quickly, as would be evident when one accepts the end result of it. Possibility number two was finally abandoned. It was felt that the cost of meeting and overcoming established competition in direct selling to the retailers would be excessive. Possibility number three was accepted and a new company was formed with a nominal capital.
>
> The decision then was to open fifteen stores as quickly as reasonably possible. This number was fixed as the maximum which could be controlled from headquarters without the added cost of 'area managers'. Then it was agreed that all fifteen stores should be within a restricted area –no need to say why for it was obvious.
>
> We advertised for a general manager, and after careful selection (in which we used a form of intelligence test, which I won't describe because it would now be out-moded) we hired a man with experience in chain store operation. I think it was his practical hard work that made me appreciate that no plan, however well conceived, can be successful unless the people to operate it can measure up to the responsibility. The business grew and made good profits.

Aided by articles and broadcasts as well as his book *Principles of Salesmanship* written in 1917, Whitehead's reputation grew. By 1924 he had so much consultancy work that he became a Professor part-time and soon afterwards set himself up as a fully fledged management consultant. Subsequent clients included the United Drug Co. Inc. and J. C. Penney, who publicized his work for them; and also the Boston Consolidated Gas Co. who did not offer a public recommendation, but whose private reference to his work was to have far-reaching consequences.

Whitehead returned to London in 1929 for personal reasons and with the intention of giving up consultancy work for good. Presumably he did not think there would be a demand for his type of service in the very different business climate in Britain. However, within a month of getting home, he was invited to visit the head of the British Commercial Gas Association who had written to America for suggestions about training methods for gas salesmen. As a result of the work Whitehead had done for Boston his name was given to this man.

Whitehead recalled that when he said he had finished with management consulting, the reply was: 'Do you think it fair to come to your own country with all that knowledge and not let us have the benefit of it?' The appeal made him change his mind – so he was back in consultancy.

The Gas contract was followed by several others. Then came a request from Earl Attlee (then Mr Attlee) who was Postmaster General to advise on business organization and sales training for the then infant telephone service. Work for other Government services followed.

Dr Whitehead died in November 1974, aged 94, after a career in management consulting which spanned more than 50 years. In addition to starting his own company, Harold Whitehead & Partners in London, he was appointed a founder member of the British Institute of Management's Council and made an Honorary Fellow of the Institute of Management Consultants, a distinction only awarded to consultants who are considered to have given outstanding service to the profession.

The Entrepreneur

Most famous of the early management consultants, whose activities took pre-war London by storm, however, was a buccaneering French-born American, Charles E. Bedaux. Bedaux's personal flamboyance combined with blockbusting business tactics resulted in widespread publicity, but won him no professional honours or Government patrons. Instead, for many years, he has been considered something of a skeleton in management consulting cupboards. Nevertheless, the business he founded in Britain in 1926 has acted as a direct launching pad for four of the largest consulting groups practising in Britain today, and has influenced many others indirectly.

Described by a contemporary as 'assuredly not the scientific type, but rather the promoter and entrepreneur', Bedaux operated on a much larger scale than any of his contemporaries, recruiting and training hundreds of consultants and operating simultaneously internationally and in many companies. A small man, with a large head, Bedaux had one of those 'rags to riches' life stories which all American businessmen love to hear. Born in Paris in 1886, he received some technical training as an engineer before emigrating to New York at the age of twenty with little money and no English. His early days in his adopted country were spent doing a succession of menial jobs, including washing up dishes in a New York restaurant. He went on from there to become a 'ground hog' or member of a construction team building a tunnel under the Hudson River before moving on to Cleveland, Ohio, and setting up as a consultant.

By this time he had developed into an extremely well-dressed, suave, and urbane individual. He could put his arguments across with great effectiveness in English which was perfect though with a pronounced, and very attractive, French accent.

The 'B' unit comes to Britain

The basis for Bedaux's consulting was the concept of a common unit which could be applied to the evaluation of any type of work. It was intended to provide an objective standard on which to base financial incentive schemes and by which different types of work could be compared. It was described nearly fifty years later by Russell Curry, the first president of the Institute of Work Study, as a development of Taylor's time study but with an important refinement. Previously, time study had been composed simply of the average elapsed time for each element. Bedaux introduced a new factor, rating assessment. As each element was timed, the time study man assessed a rating value for the speed and effectiveness with which the element was carried out. Thus a serious attempt was made to bring a qualitative element into time study. Furthermore, Bedaux followed Gilbreth's conception of introducing a rest allowance for the recovery from fatigue into the basic calculations of a B (or Bedaux) unit value.

Using his unit of measurement, Bedaux was soon able to demonstrate to industrialists that major increases in productivity, increases in hourly earnings, and reductions in unit costs could be achieved without substantial additions to capital expenditure. Gilbreth is said to have had enough gall to walk into a factory like the Zeiss works in Germany or the Pierce Arrow plant in the United States and announce that he could speed up production by one-fourth, and then proceed to do it. Bedaux claimed, and achieved, even more spectacular improvements. An average taken over a number of years is said to have achieved a 40 per cent increase in worker productivity, a 20 per cent decrease in unit labour costs and a 12½ per cent increase in hourly earnings.

As with all the early work measurement activities, the controls developed as part of the system provided both workers and management with daily information about performance and losses. The fact that the basis on which the calculations were made was kept a closely guarded secret and shrouded in mystique only added to the appeal of the formula for industrialists.

The Bedaux consultancy flourished, and at the age of 38, he was operating from palatial offices on the southern tip of Manhattan Island in a building overlooking a park and with a view covering most of the incoming shipping lanes. Backed by its inventor's considerable personal magnetism and promotional flair the system not only produced remarkable results, but also became something of a cult amongst American blue-chip companies in the 1920s and early 1930s. In Rochester, New York, for instance, which had about half a million inhabitants in 1924, it was estimated that about 25 companies were using the Bedaux system. When applying for new jobs, workers in the area would quote their 'Bedaux' record in their previous jobs as a recommendation.

Magnetism and mystique

Among the increasingly large American companies which flocked to Bedaux's offices at this period was Kodak; and it was work for this client which first took Bedaux and his consulting methods to Britain. Here he found a trading environment and tradition which was very different from that which he was used to. The early 1920s was a time of rapid industrial expansion in the United States. Trade union influence, except in a few industries, was weak. Emphasis was placed on securing increased productivity both from new equipment and through better manpower control.

What Bedaux stubbornly refused to appreciate was that not only were jobs at a premium in Britain, but the trade union movement, having demonstrated its strength during the General Strike of 1926, the year Bedaux set up his British company, was able to put up organized resistance to employment cuts. By the early 1930s, industrial depression had forced national unemployment up to nearly 20 per cent while in particular communities, such as Wales, the figure rose to a peak of more than 70 per cent.

It is not surprising that the 'Bedaux System' which could result in the number of jobs being halved met with strong opposition from workers and their representatives. Dislike of the system was not confined to its effects but also included its method of implementation. Consultants working for Bedaux remembered fifty years later that they were regarded with hatred and scorn by factory workers. One recalled having to have a police escort in order to enter and leave a Birmingham factory safely during this period. Timing was often done secretly. Stopwatches were disguised as ordinary wristwatches and peepholes cut in office walls so that factory workers could be watched surreptitiously.

Undoubtedly one of the problems was inept introduction of the system by the British managers of the day, many of whom shared Bedaux's own lack of sensitivity. Employers had a wide choice in filling vacancies and could choose the best people for each job. Anyone who failed to become a good operator could easily be sacked. Because of the high unemployment, workers were afraid to lose their jobs and they made the maximum effort for the sake of security of employment.

Colwell J. Carney, who trained with Bedaux in New York and moved to England to become managing director of the British company, was not impressed by his first impression of a British client. In a short history of the Charles E. Bedaux Company up to 1936 written for internal circulation, he recorded that after an hour's presentation of the system which forecast a 60 per cent reduction in unit labour costs, the managing director of the client company 'merely smiled slightly, and indicated that his understanding was that Bedaux was something like Eno's Fruit salts to be taken by industry'.

Welfare workers and medical personnel as well as union leaders were suspicious about the impact the new productivity techniques might have on health. They remained unconvinced even after one of Bedaux's largest clients, Imperial Chemical Industries, took the concerns seriously enough to conduct detailed research into potential health problems. Using controlled groups working on the Bedaux system and similar groups of workers matched by age, type of work and general conditions 'not on Bedaux', ICI was able to give a clean bill of health to the work requirements of the standards. Bedaux consultants claimed in vain that increasing output from the equivalent of three man hours a day to six man hours a day still allowed ample time for worker's rest, personal needs and for unavoidable delays even though it represented a 100 per cent increase in productivity.

Moreover, productivity increases did not invariably lead to losses of jobs. One of Bedaux's achievements was in pioneering the reduction in working hours from a 47 hour week to a 40 hour week. Colwell Carney recalls that this came about as follows:

> One of our clients during this period was Mander Brothers of Wolverhampton. Their factories produced paints, varnishes, inks, dry colours and tin cans. It was in co-operation with the management of this company that we introduced the first 40 hour week. This was done in close co-ordination between the Mander Brothers' Board of Directors and trade union representatives. This work received the personal attention of Ernest Bevin and the scheme was negotiated with him at Transport House in London. Substantial increases in workers' earnings were achieved, even though hours were reduced from a previous average of 47 hours per week to 40 hours per week. A different scheme was introduced at the works of J. & J. Colman at Norwich. Here the reduction in hours per week was from 44 to 40, with somewhat higher earnings obtaining at the lower level of hours worked.

Carney recalls that if the emphasis on output in the system Bedaux promoted and marketed was severe as far as the workers involved were concerned, it was equally severe on the consultants who were employed by Bedaux. The schedule for payment for Bedaux consultants in the United States was as follows:

In training	$300 per month.
On assignments	
1st six months	$3.00 per hour worked, invoiced and paid for by the client.
2nd six months	$3.50 per hour worked, invoiced and paid for by the client.
3rd six months	$4.00 per hour worked, invoiced and paid for by the client.

Thereafter as a resident consultant.

Commission granted for new business amounted to 10 per cent of fees. These were invoiced to the client at the rate of $10.00 per hour, or approximately 20 times the average hourly earnings for male factory workers at that time. No payment was made for time lost because of illness, vacations or unassigned time. Nevertheless, during 1927, it was possible for a consultant to earn more than $11,000 per annum under these schedules, big money indeed in the 1920s in England! In addition, extra payments were made for training new men. The earnings were based upon more than 2,500 hours worked at a rate of $4.00 per hour. Under this system, a director could earn up to $10,000 per annum.

The British Bedaux Company flourished. A number of well-known British companies including the Persian Oil Company (now British Petroleum), Huntley & Palmer, and Avon Rubber joined ICI as clients of the consultancy service. From these, work spread further afield to, for example, Africa, Estonia, and Portugal.

Social gaffes

Bedaux's personal fortunes rose with that of his business. He maintained a lavish style of living, travelled a great deal and enjoyed the delights of the fashionable London season. A wide circle of high society friends and acquaintances included no less a celebrity than the Duke of Windsor, who loved America and the company of American businessmen. Bedaux also knew Mrs Simpson and is said to have introduced the Duke to her.

The friendship became a matter for public speculation when the Duke and Duchess accepted Bedaux's offer of his magnificent sixteenth century Château de Cande at Touraine in France as the venue for their wedding; and the vehement, almost hysterical, indignation against Mrs Simpson and everything associated with her which swept through Britain attacked him also.

Bedaux blindly refused to believe that the Duke's abdication in 1936 would be permanent. Colwell Carney records that both he and the Vice Chairman were as unsuccessful in their attempts to persuade him that the Duke would not be reinstated by popular acclaim as they were in persuading him that his analysis of the British economic structure was mistaken. Bedaux, who by now was spending most of his time in France, did however agree to the British company being financially restructured in 1936. The proposals to restructure into what became Associated Industrial Consultants (now Inbucon) stemmed from increasing concern by the directors about the fact that three-quarters of the ownership of the company rested with Bedaux and other nonresident associates. The directors and senior consultants were alarmed about the absence of job security, and even more so about their inability to modify operating policies to meet local conditions. Their recommendation to Bedaux that a holding company be formed with the resident directors taking effective control was accepted.

Long term employment agreements were reached with the resident directors; and Norman Pleming, who later became a leading figure in professional management circles, was elected to head up the new board.

The reorganization took place none too soon. For Bedaux's activities were to become an even deeper source of embarrassment to his successors. With companies in Germany and France as well as Britain, Bedaux had become an admirer of early Nazi experiments in industrial reorganization. He was friendly with General Goering and is said to have been behind the Duke and Duchess's visit to inspect low-cost housing in Germany in 1937 and the Duke's meeting with Hitler.

Even though there was, as yet, no war fever in England, Anglo-German relationships had become very cool and the Duke's visit did not go down well in England. Public dislike of Bedaux and his system had by now reached a peak in the United States as well as in Britain. Contemporary reports describe the Bedaux method 'of speeding up work in factories' as 'inhuman'. Fear of demonstrations by American labour representatives forced the cancellation of a trip by the Duke and Duchess to America to see low-cost housing and industrial installations once it was generally realized that Bedaux had made the arrangements.

Bedaux happened to be in France at the time of the Dunkirk evacuation and not only stayed there during the German occupation of that country but carried on trading. It is doubtful if there was any ideological motivation behind his decision to collaborate with the Vichy Government – he said later that he considered the Germans 'were the only people left to do business with in occupied France' – nevertheless it was something which his colleagues back in London found hard to forgive.

He continued to work closely with the Germans even after the United States came into the war, and eventually was arrested by the American army in North Africa while working on an elaborate scheme to lay pipes across two thousand miles of the Sahara from Central Africa. He was flown back to America and, after many delays, the Department of Justice investigated his career and his legal position before telling him that he would be charged with treason and trading with the enemy. In 1944 he committed suicide by taking an overdose of sleeping tablets.

3
The Golden Years

By September 1939, when Britain declared war on Germany, the principles of management consultancy were well established. Not only industrialists but also government departments were starting to realize that the improvements in output which could be achieved were no mere fluke. A number of firms other than Bedaux had come into the field and were, by now, using methods which were less controversial but still produced remarkable increases in productivity.

Of considerable help in making management consultants more acceptable was a recovery in the economy dating from the mid 1930s which brought an easing in unemployment. Although some of the basic industries such as textiles, particularly cotton, were hit by overseas competition, new industries – notably motor vehicles and electrical goods – were expanding and creating new jobs to replace those which had become obsolete. The fact that more consultants were consciously adopting a consensus approach to industrial relations was also beneficial in easing the hostile attitudes which were a legacy from the unfavourable publicity connected with Bedaux.

The Gilbreths were early exponents of worker participation through joint employer-employee councils whose ideas were spreading across the Atlantic, more subtly and in a different way from those of Bedaux, but just as effectively.

After her husband's death in 1924 the remarkable Mrs Gilbreth concentrated on teaching the principles of motion study she had jointly developed with him. One of her pupils was Anne Shaw (1904–1982), a Scottish girl who was to become one of the leading British practitioners of management consultancy. Daughter of

Helen B. Shaw, Unionist MP for Bothwell in Lanarkshire, Anne Shaw read mathematics, psychology and social science at Edinburgh University. After graduating in 1927, she won a scholarship for European women to Bryn Mawr College in Philadelphia. There, she met Lillian Gilbreth, studied under her as a management research assistant, and developed such a close personal relationship with the family that she was nicknamed the thirteenth child.

First of the disciples

Returning home in 1930 with the intention of applying for a permanent residency in America, Anne Shaw was instead persuaded to join Metropolitan Vickers in Manchester as Supervisor of Women in the Meter Department. A motion study started at the women's employment department gradually developed until it covered the whole of the group which at the time employed upwards of 50,000 workers. Anne Shaw's remarkable achievement was to introduce the concept of motion study by negotiating change with works committees and trade union representatives – a revolutionary idea in Britain in the 1930s, but one which produced results. Improvement in production per worker reached by up to 175 per cent.

Training courses were organized for motion study engineers from each factory in the group and the type of motion study taught and developed was in the direct Gilbreth tradition.

Like many other employers at that time, Metropolitan Vickers' policy towards women employees was to dispense with their services when they married. Anne Shaw's contribution was sufficiently well recognized that when she married in 1937, she was encouraged to stay on – provided she retained her maiden name!

Other forces were at work to harmonize industrial relations in Britain. The Boys' Welfare Association (forerunner of the Industrial Society) had been campaigning not only for improved working conditions but also for improved relationships between trade unions and management since 1918. A founder patron of the Association was Seebohm Rowntree, managing director of Rowntree's of York, a firm famous even then for its progressive employment policies.

The management movement

A Rowntree disciple who was to have a profound effect on management consulting was Lyndall Fownes Urwick. Born in 1891 the son of a nobleman – a factor of great significance in the class-conscious society of prewar Britain – Urwick directly influenced many generations of managers and consultants through his lectures and writings as well as through the company he founded in 1934. Urwick was a prolific and outspoken supporter of scientific management, long before management itself was accepted as a profession.

He has written or edited, either by himself or with others, more than 40 books and booklets on subjects dealing with management and had more than 200 articles published. The best known of his books are probably *The Elements of Administration* and *Leadership in the Twentieth Century*. Urwick's unique contribution, however, was in winning public recognition for management as a profession through work on committees and in government departments at a critical point in its development.

In an article published in 1969 when he was aged 78 entitled 'Letter to an MBA', he vividly describes how he was inspired in his formative years both by Frederick Taylor's thinking and by his own experiences during the First World War:

> We all want to 'make something' of ourselves. But how do we set about it? I was heir to a great family glove manufacturing business but I didn't want merely to make money. I wanted to make money legitimately, because I was doing something that was useful to my society.
>
> I took a history degree at Oxford (no business schools in Great Britain in 1910). Then, just as I'd started to learn about the business, the first World War came. I was a Reserve 2nd Lt and my battalion was one 2nd Lt short, so I was in the first day's fighting. Today I'm still here, with all my limbs. The chances of this happening were about one in 500.
>
> Some months after August, 1914, an officer with whom I was working said to me 'If you survive this war, which I admit at the moment seems improbable, and go back to your family business, you ought to read a book called *Shop Management*. It's by an American engineer named Taylor. He can't write for nuts, but he's got something.'

Urwick read the book while he was sheltering in some shattered stables of the chateau at Hooge on the Menin Road. 'That was it!' he recalls. 'It answered the problem which had worried me at Oxford, how to reconcile a business career with being useful to society. It made of management "an intelligent occupation". I determined then and there that if I survived I would devote my life to management.'

At the end of the war, after a further two years in the family firm, Urwick went to Rowntree's in York, as organizing secretary, where, of course, he was to meet another idealist in Seebohm Rowntree. He became a fervent admirer of Rowntree, describing him many years later as the 'first British employer to see clearly that the first duty of a manager is to manage effectively, whatever other ideals and aspirations he may cherish'. Urwick wholeheartedly embraced Rowntree's beliefs that two conditions were needed before any large group of human beings could be expected to co-operate effectively for any purpose.

These conditions were: first, that the group knows and understands what the purpose is and accepts it as a desirable purpose socially; second, that it is satisfied that the arrangements for co-operation are as well designed as is humanly possible, to safeguard not only the interests of the group but the individual aims, aspirations and feelings of each person composing the group. The Cocoa Works at York in those days were a kind of 'practical university of management', Urwick recalls.

Nevertheless, in 1928 after six years with the company, he left at the age of 37. 'I was offered the only international post in management worth having – the Directorship of the International Management Institute at Geneva. And I was still dreaming my dream.'

Urwick found the work at Geneva fascinating but it was not to last. The Institute was closed down, suddenly, in 1933. Hitler had come into power in Germany and the chief backer of the Institute, an American, withdrew from all his European commitments at short notice. 'So back I went to London, where I was "That chap Urwick. Ran some queer show in Geneva, management or something. Failed of course." I looked around and decided that the only way to go on working at management and to make a decent living was to start a management consulting business.'

When war was declared, consulting had sufficient status to be declared a reserved occupation. Even so, one ex-consultant remembers wanting to leave his manufacturing employer to join a consultancy and being refused twice by the Government tribunal set up under the Direction of Labour legislation on the grounds that his new work was only equal in importance to his old work. Eventually he was allowed to change, but was required for his first nine months as a consultant to make weekly 'servicing visits' to his old employer (at the latter's expense).

Although the 1914–18 war had given some impetus to new industrial ideas, these had soon petered out in peacetime. A few investigations of motion study were carried out by the Industrial Fatigue Research Board which developed from an earlier committee dealing with the health of munition workers, but these were not widely publicized. Later, in 1921, the National Institute of Industrial Psychology skirted around the question of motion or movement study, but its work was restricted and again not widely adopted by industrialists. British companies which were interested in pursuing the idea were put off by the lack of trained motion study investigators. Few were willing to pay for a training which was expensive and which in most cases could be obtained only in the United States.

Government patronage

The outbreak of the Second World War brought a sharp revival in official interest. An unremitting drive for output at almost any cost was the main task of the huge central planning machine set up by the Coalition Cabinet led by Sir Winston Churchill. Few businesses of any size escaped requisitioning of their premises by various authorities. Metropolitan Vickers turned to manufacturing armaments; and the motion study techniques being used there and the results they achieved quickly caught the attention of Sir Stafford Cripps, the wartime minister responsible for aircraft production.

In 1942, Cripps formed a Production Efficiency Board and asked for Anne Shaw to be seconded to it to advise him on the best utilization of labour in the aircraft industry.

Later she was joined by Nancy Seear (later the Baroness Seear), and set up a Personnel Advisory Service which introduced training schemes for motion study in factories along the lines of those organized at Vickers and using training facilities and staff loaned by the company.

Some of the improved methods developed as a result of these courses were collected in a demonstration organized by the Ministry of Aircraft Production in 1945, with the object of interesting other industries in the peacetime applications of motion study as a means of increasing output per operator. While the demonstration did not produce an overwhelming response from manufacturers, the training schemes which preceded it at least created a body of trained and experienced investigators which was dispersed at the end of the war into many different industries and organizations. In this way the Gilbreth tradition permeated large areas of industry even if it was often unrecognized as such.

Postwar reconstruction

In 1945, the Labour Government which was elected by the returning soldiers and a tired nation looked to managers and management consultants for help in reconstructing the shattered industrial base. Cripps, initially as president of the Board of Trade, and from 1947 as Chancellor of the Exchequer, created a framework which set the pace for the expansion in management and management services including consulting, which lasted for the next 25 years.

During his term in the postwar Labour cabinet, which lasted from 1945 to 1950, Cripps introduced a number of significant measures. He set up two committees. One explored the field and established the case for a central institute in which all interests concerned with improving management should find a focus. This was chaired by Sir Cecil Weir. The second committee, under Sir Clive Baillieu, then President of the Federation of British Industries (later to become the Confederation of British Industry) was charged with advising on the steps to be taken to form such an institute. Shortly afterwards, Cripps announced that it was the Government's intention to sponsor the foundation of this institute and to make grants of up to £150,000 for the purpose to be spread over five years.

The move was by no means uncritically received. Not all industrialists welcomed the prospect of an institute for professional management, particularly if it meant rubbing shoulders with trade unionists. There was considerable, though discreet, dissent in boardrooms behind the scenes. Nevertheless, by September 1947 the British Institute of Management had started active life and its inaugural meeting was held less than six months later, on Wednesday, 21 April 1948.

A management body

The significance of the formation of the British Institute of Management was that it set an official seal on management as a profession vital to British industry. Before the war, and indeed for many years afterwards, the bulk of British manufacturing industry had consisted of proprietors and operatives. The clerks, who were in many instances the nearest equivalent to modern management, were not encouraged to think independently. Their task was to carry out orders emanating from the Board of directors. The concept of democratic management and of associating workers in the development of company policy propounded by Cripps, a committed Socialist, has not been universally accepted, even today.

The Institute had a profound effect in widening horizons in the early years, despite the suspicion and distrust with which it was regarded by some trade unionists as well as employers. The impact of some of the productivity missions it sponsored to the United States to look at developments in budgeting and accounting, for instance, is still remembered.

In addition to encouraging the adoption of scientific management methods, Cripps gave a specific boost to management consultants by inviting four distinguished practitioners to sit on the Institute's first Council, and encouraging others to participate in the various satellite subcommittees. Lt.-Col. Lyndall Urwick was one of two vice-chairmen of the Council and there is no doubt but that he played a large part, behind the scenes, in its formation.

Urwick not only had the ear of industrialists – Sir Charles Renold of Renold Chains who was the first chairman of the Institute's Council, was one of Urwick's first clients – he also had the ear of Government.

During the war, Urwick accepted (foolishly, he said afterwards) an offer to join the Treasury Investigating Section. He felt that his side of consulting – top organization and clerical methods – was likely to be quiescent in wartime, adding that 'Anyway I wanted to do a national job'. The Treasury landed Urwick with two very frustrating years. 'I succeeded in forcing them to start the Treasury Organization and Methods Division. But I had to play so much "politics" in doing it that I was poison in the eyes of the Head of Civil Service,' he said afterwards. At the end of the two years Urwick went back into uniform as Chief of the Staff to the Petroleum Warfare Department working on FIDO (clearing fog from airfields) and PLUTO (the pipeline for fuel laid under the English Channel). In 1944 he was appointed chairman of the Government committee which published the Urwick Report on education for management in 1947. As a result of this report the joint British Institute of Management and Ministry of Education scheme for education in management at technical colleges was set up.

A guide to consultants

Urwick was by far the most prominent public figure among the management consultants of his day. But the other practitioners on the Council, Harold Whitehead, Oliver Roskill and T. G. Rose, had very high personal reputations. Working further off stage was Norman Pleming who had been elected to the Board of the British Bedaux Company in 1936 (later Inbucon/AIC), and chaired a special committee set up as one of the first actions of the Institute 'to investigate ways by which reliable information as to management and industrial consultants can be made available'. Later a permanent committee was set up to operate a Register of Consultants, and by October 1948 a circular letter and printed questionnaires had been sent out inviting consultants to participate.

As is recorded in the Institute's first annual report, the Register Committee was formed 'as a result of suggestions from the Government and other quarters'. What is not recorded are the concerns which led to the suggestions. People who attended the early meetings recall that there were complaints about salesmen, particularly of office equipment, who described themselves as independent consultants to get introductions to prospective purchasers.

The strong views held by L. O. Russell, the first director of the Institute, were probably shared by many of his contemporaries. Russell recalled, in a speech given to the Office Management Association in 1949, that when he was working in a publishing office in the 1920s and 1930s he had to develop his ideas about office work 'by the light of nature, and I may say, in the face of considerable scepticism and resistance. There was no authoritative organization, no established body of knowledge, to which I could turn for enlightenment, or to provide support for my ideas. I was the victim of the purveyors of many types of patent system – for which there was no way of knowing about them without going to the expense of trying them out.' There were also abuses in the employment field with so-called 'independent' consultants seeking commissions from both employer and applicant.

However, the main concern, even then, seems to have been about incompetence rather than dishonesty. The thousands of ex-servicemen who were being demobbed at the time had to be re-established in civilian life. One of the fears was that some would set themselves up as management consultants even though they held no qualifications. The register was seen as a way of helping both industrialists and established consultants by providing a recommendation of competence.

Sponsored experiments

Another move by the postwar government which encouraged the development of the consulting profession was the sponsorship of experiments to improve productivity in the textile industry. One of the projects specifically referred to by Cripps in his speech at the inaugural meeting of the British Institute of Management concerned the Musgrave cotton spinning mill at Bolton in Lancashire.

The Musgrave trial, completed between January and July 1947, was carried out by The P–E Consulting Group for the Labour Department of the Cotton Board. It was accepted by the operatives and the local trade union on the basis that first, there would be no reduction in the existing level of earnings; and second, there would be complete freedom to revert afterwards to the original methods of working if operatives wished to do so. The conditions of acceptance are interesting in that they illustrate the reservations the shop floor workers of the day had about productivity schemes in general.

By a combination of reallocating operatives' duties, rearranging machines, and introducing some new equipment, the consultants were able to increase production per man hour by 39 per cent. The total number of operatives was reduced by 21 per cent from 39 to 31, while the weekly earnings of those who remained rose by 30 per cent as a result of an incentive bonus scheme. Despite the reduction in the length of the working week from 48 to 45 hours which took place during the progress of the trial, there was also an increase in the supervision and relaxation time from 27 to 34 per cent.

The experiment was considered to be a success by all concerned.

A full report showing how the results were achieved was published by the Board in May 1948 and was given a great deal of publicity. Another event which caught the public eye at about this time was the publication in 1949 of *Cheaper by the Dozen*, a humorously written semi-biography of the Gilbreth family by two of the twelve children. Although a flippant account of American family life, the book is packed with factual examples of motion study in action. This became a bestseller, in Britain as well as the United States, and undoubtedly had some influence on the boom in demand which consultants experienced in the late 1950s and 1960s. A mark of official British recognition of the Gilbreths' contribution to management was that Dr Lillian Gilbreth was elected the first Honorary Fellow of the British Institute of Management in 1951.

Despite the tremendous wartime and postwar boost, the early 1950s were not an easy time for consultants. There had been three or four years of breathless expansion during which the established consulting firms recruited extensively from among the ranks of ex-servicemen. These were men who, although still in their twenties, had been matured and toughened by wartime responsibilities. However in many cases they had only slight industrial experience and had to be trained not only in the skills of their craft but also to adjust to civilian working conditions. In 1952, the profession lost a powerful patron in Westminster with the death of Sir Stafford Cripps. Urwick gave up executive consulting work in 1951 and stepped down from the British Institute of Management's Council the following year.

'In 1951 I was 60,' he wrote, 'and I think at 60 one should "get out of the boys' hair". So I bought a house in the country and dropped back to Chairman of the Board only. I went to London one day a week, while I was in England. When I hit 70 [1961] I decided to come and live in Australia. That was purely personal: my wife wanted to live here. I've remained a Director of the company and I visit them in England once or twice a year.'

Urwick remained in close touch with events after his retirement. Shortly before his move to Australia he said that he regarded the distance from Australia to England as he regarded the distance from London to Inverness in the days when he first started because of advances in rapid air travel. Inevitably though, his retirement brought a feeling of loss.

At Urwick Orr, where he had been Managing Partner as well as

Chairman, there was a gap of three years before William Coutts Donald took over as chief executive. Fears of a third world war caused by the Korean conflict had a disturbing effect on demand for consultancy services. The early 1950s were years of consolidation and in some cases disillusionment in management generally. But by 1953, once the Korean ceasefire agreement had been signed, there was an almost immediate improvement in the industrial environment and hence in demand for consultancy work.

The boom begins

By 1956, it was estimated that there were over 1000 experienced consultants at work, about two-thirds of whom were either engineers or accountants. This was the period when there was an almost blind belief in unlimited and unending growth. The next decade and a half were an exhilarating period for industry characterized by the famous slogan 'You've never had it so good' used by Harold Macmillan in the 1959 General Election campaign. Once they were unleashed from wartime restrictions, consumers clamoured for the new fabrics and textiles, for convenience foods, domestic electrical appliances, furniture, and motor cars. The newly christened 'teenagers' were emerging as a powerful pressure group. Along with their heroes like Elvis Presley, the rock-and-roll performer, they started a new industry in pop music and gramophones.

Consultants were given bigger and bigger assignments particularly in production control. An example of this was the design and staffing of a completely new factory which the P–E Consulting Group carried out from scratch in 1955. The project concerned Tufted Carpets, a company formed by five leading carpet manufacturers to make carpets by a process which had already been developed in America but was new to Britain. The work involved market research, technical design, supervision of the design, manufacture and delivery of plant, recruitment of staff; in short, all the processes needed to get a new factory underway.

The four biggest established consulting groups, The P–E Consulting Group, PA Management Consultants, Urwick Orr, and Inbucon accounted for about three-quarters of all the consulting work done and expanded their activities in all directions. New divisions and departments were added at a breathtaking pace.

Marketing became an important activity with the emphasis on advertising as restrictions on newsprint were lifted and innovations in colour printing were made. The first television commercial was broadcast in the United Kingdom in September 1955. In the United States, advertising agencies were being urged to recognize themselves as 'advanced laboratories in psychology'. The popularity of Vance Packard's *The Hidden Persuaders*, published in 1957, indicated that a peak had been reached. In Britain, the first Professor of Marketing was appointed in 1965 as the result of a joint exercise between the Institute of Marketing and Lancaster University.

Consultants had been in the marketing arena much earlier. They themselves will readily admit that they do not always get their timing right, but their stock in trade is in spotting trends which will bring changes. Roger Falk, who had previously been Director General of the British Export Trade Research Organisation, joined The P–E Consulting Group to establish a marketing development subsidiary in 1952: PA Management Consultants set up a sales and marketing division a year later.

Recruitment became an important activity in the boom years of the late 1950s and early 1960s when labour was scarce. PA Management Consultants set up a division to recruit senior executives for clients in 1957 – a year before the *Daily Telegraph* carried its first displayed recruitment advertisements. Desperate personnel officers had to find ways and means of making certain their advertisements were seen and read, and demand for the new service was high. For PA and other management consultants who followed their lead, work in this area had the additional advantage that they could publicize their name without infringing professional rules as well as providing a service to clients.

Expansion and diversification

With so many activities under their umbrellas two of the big consulting groups felt that their original trading names were too restrictive and both adopted American style initials. Production Engineering changed its name to the P–E Consulting Group in 1965, while Personnel Administration became PA Management Consultants at about the same time.

The 1960s were halcyon days for management consultants.

Recruits still had higher educational qualifications than their counterparts in industry. There was plenty of money for training and supervision so that the consultants' expertise was kept up to date. Clients were queuing up at the doors of the established consultancies seeking help with a wide variety of problems.

Most of the consulting firms at this time wanted well-rounded general consultants on their staffs. They pushed their consultants, whatever their original disciplines, into tackling all types of assignment, relying on supervisors to ensure an adequate standard of performance. This meant that personnel specialists and accountants for instance worked on factory production problems, while engineers could be involved in solving marketing questions.

One leading consultant recalls that, about this time, nearly every consultant would be expected to be able to run a course for salesmen, whereas now, it would be carried out by specialists. 'I'm not an accountant,' he adds, 'but I was doing some work for a company and one of the things I turned up was that their management accounting procedures were just not giving them any useful information at all. So I stopped what I was doing, and, for six weeks worked on getting their management accounting procedures right. Today, I don't think I would be allowed to do this, partly because there are much more sophisticated approaches to these things available and partly because one would be using advanced technologies.'

Many of the consultants operating at this time found the variety of tasks stimulating. They enjoyed the challenge, felt they had benefited from it, and mostly felt they did a competent job.

This was the period of what one commentator has described as 'merger mania'. The 1960s saw a spate of giant industrial and commercial amalgamations such as the merger between GEC and AEI, Trust Houses and Charles Forte, Cadbury with Schweppes, Rowntree with Mackintosh. Between 1961 and 1968, mergers reduced the number of manufacturing companies of assets of £500,000 and over by nearly one-third. Major restructuring of organizations was the order of the day and management consultants were frequently called in to help.

The halcyon sixties
By the beginning of the 1960s, management consultants had

become the glamorous crown princes of the industrial world. Having, they believed, firmly shed their old title of industrial engineers, they had become a fashion whose help was being solicited by every imaginable type of organization.

The ebullient self-confidence and innocent belief in unending prosperity and gradual change are illustrated by the symbols adopted by the newly formed Institute of Management Consultants at this time. The coat of arms has a sun in splendour signifying the overall approach of consultants with a cogwheel inside to signify industry and business. Also included is a gold cornucopia to signify plenty or prosperity and a white fesse with ten black dots to represent a punched tape (long since outmoded), for input to electronic computers.

The self-confidence appeared justified in that it was matched by revenue figures. Combined fee income recorded by the Management Consultants Association notched up annual increases of over 20 per cent in the late 1960s – a truly impressive growth rate at a time when inflation was running at less than 5 per cent. Recruitment into the big consulting firms soared as even the flood of bright young graduates who were flocking into the industry was insufficient to meet the apparently insatiable demand from clients. The number of consultants employed by the Association's members which stood at 1,530 at the beginning of 1964 had more than doubled by early 1970.

Clouds on the horizon

With hindsight, consultants blame themselves for becoming too 'cerebral' (and also too arrogant) during this period. Senior consultants tended to distance themselves from fee-earning activities. They overdelegated to the more junior staffs which were flooding into the consultancies. They were more concerned with administration and supervision than with rolling up their sleeves and working alongside their clients.

In fairness, similar accusations of remoteness have been made about the managements of the period. There was a tendency to apply the same techniques, the same blanket solution to every situation irrespective of its local characteristics. This was the era when the chain stores made every High Street look identical. Although a reaction had started in the United States, in Britain it was the heyday of the multinational. Every company wanted to make itself look as big as possible. Many organizations called in management consultants simply because it was the fashion. They had little idea how consultants operate or what they expected to achieve. Some grand consultants' schemes were never implemented, others were poorly executed as a result.

End of an era
When the collapse came, it did so very suddenly, taking everyone by surprise. 'We had virtually all of our staff employed, a number of big jobs going. Within literally three months in 1970, a number of our jobs were cancelled and there was no continuing work. It was as abrupt as that,' was how the managing director of one consulting firm described it.

Instead of the 15–20 per cent increase in business which was confidently expected, 1970–71 brought a drop of about 10 per cent in consultants' fee incomes. In organizations as highly geared to fees as consultancies, the effects were traumatic. Redundancies were inevitable. The Management Consultants Association's figures for member firms' staffs record the first ever drop. The combined total of consultants employed by the big firms slumped by over a quarter between 1969–70 and 1972–73. Whole departments were chopped. A tendency towards lavish offices with marble and plush fixtures in the foyer vanished almost overnight.

If the tangible impact of the sudden drying up of consultancy contracts was severe, the psychological blow was worse. Management consultants found it difficult to adjust to the fact that one minute they were indispensable (or so it seemed) and the next they were ignored.

What had happened was that the impact of a world recession was exacerbated in Britain by a General Election and the economic policies of an inexperienced Conservative government. Immediately on taking office the 1970 Heath government abolished controls on pay and was then met with an unprecedented wave of industrial action. This started with a national docks strike which the Government chose to tackle by declaring a State of Emergency and shipping troops back from Northern Ireland. Wages were already showing signs of shooting up by an alarming 14 per cent compared with 1969–70 which, against stagnant production totals, caused a sharp drop in company profits.

The storm breaks

Industrialists slammed on their investment brakes hard in all directions. Management consultancy was only one of many services to suffer as both domestic and foreign businessmen slashed their investment programmes. At first, the setbacks were thought to be temporary, but worse was to come as the uncontrolled stampede for higher wages was fuelled by trade union resistance to the proposed industrial relations legislation.

The very grave problems which had been experienced by management consultants soon rippled throughout the industrial fabric as economic disaster followed disaster. Industrial difficulties continued with a strike by local authority workers in September 1970. More than a million working days were lost in an unofficial miners' strike. Shortly afterwards, electricity supply workers were granted an increase of around 15 per cent. However the dispute which really rocked business confidence was the eight week National Postal Workers strike which started on 19 January 1971. It was the first national postal strike ever and business was completely unprepared. Invoices, cheques, research surveys and other vital business data were all held up.

Nevertheless, few events have dealt such a savage blow to the confidence of the British business community, as the collapse of Rolls-Royce on 4 February 1971. Rolls-Royce was considered to be the pride of British quality and workmanship. The whole world gasped in amazement when it became just as bankrupt as any back street trader. There could have been no more dramatic signal to the end of an era.

Things, if anything, looked even bleaker at the start of 1972. Hardly had the New Year begun when another National Union of Mineworkers strike sparked a rota of power cuts. Vigorous, and occasionally violent picketing threatened sewage, food supplies, communications and even law and order to add to the gloom caused by the blackouts and IRA bomb scares.

Oil crisis 1973–74

Despite the expansionist budget produced by Chancellor Barber in April 1972, demand for management consultants' services had only picked up slightly, when the next blow struck eighteen months later with the quadrupling of oil prices which followed the October 1973 war in the Middle East.

There was a strong feeling of panic in the air. The Government reacted to an overtime ban and threatened strike action by miners by introducing a three day working week for manufacturing industry starting at the end of December. Many people felt that Christmas 1973 would be the last holiday they would be able to afford to enjoy.

The Conservative government was confident of victory when it called a general election for 7 February 1974, three days before the miners, by an 81 per cent majority, had voted to begin an all-out strike. Instead it lost. The first election directly precipitated by industrial action returned a Labour government, although by a narrow margin.

The stock market was in despair. Inflation was rocketing well past the previously unthinkable 10 per cent mark. Prices rose by nearly 13 per cent between January 1973 and January 1974 and kept on escalating. The Confederation of British Industry's industrial trends survey for January 1974 showed the lowest level of business confidence ever. Given industrial militancy, there seemed no chance that wage increases could be contained. Stock market indices adjusted for inflation fell during the last nine months of 1974 to a lower level than during Dunkirk, when many people thought it was unlikely that Britain would survive the war against Germany. Any management consulting firm which had not had to cut its staff in 1970–71 battened down the hatches now. Some took a double knock.

4
Consultancy Today

The explosion of interest in the computer sciences in the 1970s caught the British management consulting companies ill prepared. Up until then, the captains of industry, whom the heads of the consultancies were assiduously wooing in a bid to fight off competition from their own American rivals, were mostly content to leave computer developments to the backroom boffins. Their heads of departments, who, if they had any advanced engineering education at all, were trained in the mechanical field, were equally disinterested. The computer specialists were regarded as a race apart, operating in hermetically sealed rooms with their own obscure languages.

Suddenly, or so it seemed, the silicon chip brought what was christened New Technology (although many of the basic concepts had been around since the 1920s) onto everybody's lips. The conclusion reached by a Department of Employment study group set up in 1978 to examine the manpower implications of micro-electronics, which was 'that it will affect manufacturing industry in so many ways that it is difficult even to find a coherent framework for analysis', reflected the puzzlement of many. Coming in the midst of a period of economic crises and instability to a point where even the very basis of civilization seemed to be crumbling, the awareness that a new industrial revolution had already arrived was frightening indeed.

Computers had been in operation for a long time – what made the impact on the boardrooms was the realization that electronics had developed to a point where they could be used in the actual decision-taking processes. The DoE's study group's charting of the progress of computerization in one medium-sized mechanical engineering firm illustrates the pattern of development very vividly.

This company was identified as one which had one of the most up-to-date computer-aided manufacturing systems in the country and was likely to set the pattern for the future. Its use of computers had begun in the late 1950s for standard administrative functions in, for example, costing, accounting, and payroll work. In 1964, computerization began to move into the production control area for use in engineering bill of materials processing, and stock and production control. From this developed the use of computers in generating machine shop paperwork including work schedules for the foremen and individual cards for each machine operation. By 1970, a stock control system, information for calculation of bonuses, an actual cost system (with feedback to estimating) and progress recording/shop load information had been added.

Up to this point, what had evolved was essentially a filing and information system in which the computer was not significantly involved in making decisions. Before the end of the 1960s, however, the company decided to go a stage further and move to a data base system that could be used in actual decision-making – in such matters as whether to self-manufacture or buy in components, whether to batch and how to schedule work. The essence of the new system was to provide information on how to optimize production. The system provided immediate (real time) information on work in progress and information was brought up to date as soon as jobs were completed.

Similar and even more advanced developments in other companies and other industries were taking place simultaneously all over the world. British industrialists became aware that they would have to innovate quickly in order to keep pace with their international competitors. Bewildered, they began turning in ever growing numbers to their management consultants for help, advice and guidance – only to find, in many cases, that their confusion was mirrored by senior consultants who themselves were unable to keep pace with developments in this field.

This is not to suggest that the consultancies had not been aware of the new applications in microprocessors. All the big firms had dipped their fingers into the computer fire early, and had in many instances had them burnt because of the sluggish uptake from their clients. As early as 1958 Urwick Orr, for instance, had formed a joint subsidiary with John Diebold, the American pioneer in this area whom Lyndall Urwick had met while on a lecture tour. The subsidiary however traded at a loss for ten years until, eventually, in 1970, Urwick bought out the Diebold share and changed the company's name to Urwick Dynamics.

In the late 1960s Inbucon/AIC, the direct successor of the British Bedaux company and the oldest of the management consulting firms was taken over by Leasco, the American computer leasing company. Even if it was to fall on hard times shortly, Leasco's phenomenal growth record which gave it an increase in profits from $707,000 in 1966 to an estimated $40 million for 1969 was a clear pointer for the future. 'We're shifting from the domestic market to the European market because of the greater opportunities for profit,' Leasco's chairman Saul Steinberg, then aged 29, said when announcing the £4 million formal offer.

It was just that the timing of the interest in new technology was wrong for the consultancies. The attention of their top people was diverted towards obtaining more of the top level reorganizational work which they saw being filtered away to American rivals, like McKinsey. Further down the ladder, consultants' main drive was being channelled into a spate of productivity agreements and other industrial relations work. There were few consultants with the highly specialist knowledge needed to keep abreast of the rapid changes in the technology and even fewer with the ability to explain and interpret in broad business terms.

Even though micro-chips might be cheap, the costs of developing the software and associated hardware needed to apply microprocessors are high. The recession of the early 1970s forced consultancies to axe some of the data processing activities which, though loss making, might have provided the seed-bed for expertise. Ruefully acknowledging that they had been caught napping (like everybody else) the consultancies set to repair the gaps with extreme energy and great rapidity. Since the mid 1970s there has been a spate of amalgamations as the established consultancy firms sought assistance from smaller specialists, together with dramatic and sometimes gory internal restructurings –a symptom of which has been that three of the original 'big four' consultancies have appointed new chief executives and undergone significant management changes within the last three years. The adjustments are still underway and it is still too soon to assess the effect. However the consultancies themselves are confident that they have more than caught up any lost ground. In fact, in some cases, they believe they may have benefited from the hiccup in that they were able to bypass some of the evolutionary stages and take two jumps for the price of one.

The question of size

The only revenue which a 'pure' consulting group earns comes from its consultants' fees. The only ways this can be increased are by taking on more consultants, utilizing their time more efficiently, or increasing the fee rates charged. The disadvantage of efficient use of consultants today (in the sense that more time is devoted to fee earning activities) is that it diverts effort away from research, the fruits of which may be needed tomorrow, while competitive forces prevent fees from stepping too far out of line. The equation for size, therefore, is quite simply that of ever increasing recruitment.

While today's conditions are among the toughest ever experienced in this respect, the decision to aim singlemindedly for growth has always required a strong nerve and good timing in the consultancy business. PA achieved its present position of market leadership mainly because there was never any ambivalence by Ernest Butten, the founder, or his successors but to recruit rapidly and on a large scale. The organization started in 1943 with six consultants; seven years later there were 102. By 1963 there were 370. Today there are over 1,000 professional staff although not all of these are management consultants. New recruits were carefully selected – Butten distrusted men of independent means for instance on the grounds that 'You never know if they're going to work hard'. There were five criteria for the ideal recruit to PA in the early days. They had to be young – say 28; very ambitious, frustrated by slow progress in industry; of high but not brilliant intelligence; from a grammar school; and climbing socially from a modest home. The ideal recruit was held to be a Protestant but not a member of any particular sect – this was thought liable to distract people away from their work.

Consultants still cannot afford to be too individualistic. They have to blend into their client organizations in order to be able to observe, listen and measure. However, today, the recruiting pattern has been widened considerably in order to meet new pressures. Demand for ever more scientific knowledge in the new disciplines means that young people of, say 25, who can make an immediate contribution to a specialist team with the findings from a brand new experimental project are being engaged on the one hand. On the other, there is a demand for people in their mid-forties who have worked in industry and who understand the practical relationships in, for instance, behavioural sciences. Another change which has come with the slimming down of the traditional consultancies is that, instead of devoting their energies exclusively to administration and supervision, senior executives up to chairman level are themselves out in the field earning fees.

These changes, which have been in force since the mid-1970s, should have a profound effect on management consultancy practices of the 1980s and 1990s just as the stamp imposed by Ernest Butten and his counterparts in the late 1940s and early 1950s lasted for more than two decades.

A problem with all companies dependent exclusively on fee earning professionals is that of controlling and organizing highly skilled individuals so that they work as a team. Management consultancies are no exception, although many consultants admit privately that in tackling them they may appear like cobblers' children running about without shoes because of their reluctance to apply their sciences to their own organizations.

A policy of growth – PA

PA was unusual, not only in drawing up a structural blueprint for itself which could have come from a management consultants' textbook, but also in sticking to it. From the outset, Butten was determined first, that PA would be large; and, second, that revenues generated from management consultancy operations would be devoted to research. These twin aims were incorporated in a Charter produced on the firm's first birthday and is a remarkable example of early strategic planning. It reads as follows:

THE P.A. CHARTER
Our objective, stated in 1944 and repeated in 1953, is:
To build P.A. into the leading organisation of its kind in the world, consisting of men who are acknowledged authorities on the various branches of management, to create new and improved procedures which can be taught readily to Industrial and Commercial Staffs and

thus raise the standard of Management in the interests of the community as a whole.

The first step is to build up a Management Consulting Organisation to render beneficial service to individual firms in return for substantial fees. In this way, a growing source of revenue should be forthcoming. During the course of this consulting work, experience will be gained, the field for our work will be widened and improvements in our methods will, to a certain extent, automatically result.

With the assurance of an expanding source of revenue, the next step is to build up a Management Research Organisation, devoted to the development of New and Improved Techniques and to distribute the knowledge so gained for the benefit of all.

As new and improved Management Techniques are developed, both in quality and quantity, the services which the Consulting Organisation is able to render should be better and wider and, with its expansion, the revenue available for Research greater.

There will thus be two main sides to our work – Operating and Research. There must, however, always be the closest co-operation and liaison between these two sides and the work of each will frequently overlap.

When the Research side has established a reputation for rendering worthwhile benefits to Industry and Commerce, there is no reason why it should not be approached by individual firms, groups of firms, whole industries and even the Government to assist in solving specific problems. Fees for this work would augment the revenue derived from our Consulting Service to finance further the expanding Management Research and Development Department, Educational and Training Centres, Administrative Staff Colleges, etc.

Ernest Butten
Chairman

One of the factors which prompted Butten's departure from the new Bedaux stable where he had been since 1930 was an interest in a new training method developed by a colleague, Dr David Seymour, who then joined him when PA was formed in 1943. Seymour's approach, later known as the PA Method of Training or PAMT, produced remarkable improvements in training time and cut wastage by 50 per cent. Butten was frustrated by the failure of the Bedaux Company (which by now had changed its trading name to Associated Industrial Consultants) to exploit this training system. He was also interested in the concept of winning co-operation from workers and increasingly concerned, like many of his colleagues, about the antagonism which the Bedaux system created. Developing good relationships with the trades unions thus became an important objective from the start.

Where his own internal arrangements were concerned, Butten linked consultants' pay directly to the fees that they invoiced. Cash was desperately short in the early days and at times the company only survived through Butten's own self confidence, which as one consultant recalls, led him to work on very small (or negative) cash balances. Clients were invoiced weekly and cash collected from them within seven days – a sharp contrast to other professional practices which at the time were giving six months or more credit.

As well as a strong nerve, Butten also had luck on his side. In 1946, when the company was only three years old, a cold sales call by him on the TI Group of Companies and the resultant selling of a PAMT training assignment brought the first real break from wartime munitions factory work. Over the next seven years, consulting fees from the various members of the TI group totalled nearly £500,000 – a large sum to a consultancy firm in the 1950s. The association with TI also took PA overseas.

In 1948, at the invitation of a joint subsidiary of Stewarts & Lloyds, TI and Broken Hill Proprietary, Butten visited Australia and returned with authorization for two consultants. The Australian office which followed formed the foundation for an overseas network which currently spans 65 offices and covers 21 countries.

The seal Butten set on modern management consultancy practice ranks alongside, if very different from, that of Lyndall Urwick. Whereas Urwick led from a public platform, Butten's influence endures through the structure he created. The two men had very different backgrounds. Born on 28 July 1900, of middle (as compared with upper) class parents, Butten was nine crucial years younger than Urwick and so missed the military service which had such a profound influence on the latter.

Butten read mechanical engineering at Imperial College in London. In 1923, he joined Metropolitan Vickers as a graduate apprentice where his experience included five years in India, initially as a member of the construction staff and later as general manager of a light engineering factory. In 1930 he returned to Britain to join the Bedaux company where he was a supervising consultant in charge of five or six 'resident' consultants at the time when Leslie Orr left to join Urwick in setting up one new company and Robert Bryson left to join Maurice Lubbock in forming another. Butten, however, waited almost another ten years before making his own break. By then he had been appointed to the board of the Bedaux company which had been reorganized and re-named Associated Industrial Consultants (now Inbucon/AIC). Like Urwick, he wanted to push ahead faster and devote more resources than his co-directors would permit; and at the end of December 1942, he left to go his own way.

Like Gilbreth and Bedaux, Butten was evidently a born salesman. Contemporaries at AIC remember him as enormously enthusiastic with an ability to seize on a small incident or some modest progress, and to see it as significant, worthwhile and 'saleable'.

If a resident consultant achieved an improvement such as a 20 per cent reduction in machining time, Butten would get samples of the piece before and after the improvement and show them with real enthusiasm to the client's engineers and directors. Like Gilbreth, he was a big man physically, tall, well built and very energetic – a rugby player, steeplechase jockey and later, an excellent golfer. He is remembered, as is Bedaux, as an immaculate dresser and he insisted on similar standards throughout his company. He also, like Bedaux, paid attention to social symbols. In a recollection which, perhaps, is as revealing about the consultants of the day as it is about Butten's style of leadership, one early PA employee remembers working late in the office so Butten took him to supper at the Savoy Hotel – a place which the consultant described as being 'beyond his wildest imagination'. The same man also remembers being driven in a Rolls-Royce car for the first time on the same occasion.

Again, given the crucial nine years difference in age, Butten was able to stay very much at the helm of PA until it had weathered the postwar transition of the 1950s and 1960s and he kept a fatherly eye on its progress through the turbulent 1970s. A similar continuity in leadership was denied the P–E Consulting Group which, when Butten made his break for independence, was very much the brightest star on the management consultancy horizon.

The aristocrats – P–E

Although P–E has fewer direct connections with Bedaux than do its three contemporaries, the indirect links are very strong. The company was formed in 1934 (the same year that Orr set up in business with Urwick) by the Hon. Maurice Lubbock, youngest son of the first Lord Avebury. Educated at Eton and Balliol, Lubbock became a director of Dent, Allcroft & Co after he left Oxford. During his spell at Dent, two events occurred which influenced him in setting up the Production Engineering Company (now The P–E Consulting Group): first, the British Bedaux company was employed to install an incentive scheme, the engineer responsible for the work being Robert Bryson, who later became P–E's first managing director at the early age of 29 years. The second was a trip which Lubbock made to Canada in 1933 on behalf of Dent.

During his Canadian visit, Lubbock came into contact with the Toronto firm of J. D. Woods & Co (subsequently to be known as Woods, Gordon & Co) which were operating a comprehensive industrial consulting business. A close personal friendship sprang up between Lubbock and J. D. Woods, and the latter undertook to help in setting up a similar company in England.

Lubbock's plans had now crystallized. He returned to London and obtained the support of two friends who had been his contemporaries at Eton: W. L. Runciman, who later succeeded his father as Viscount Runciman and whose family had interests in shipping on the north-east coast; and Leo d'Erlanger, later to become a chairman and managing director of the family business of Erlangers Ltd, merchant bankers, and a channel tunnel pioneer. The shipbuilding, aircraft and motor industry contracts for blue chip clients like the De Havilland Aircraft Company, Rolls-Royce, and Hawker Aircraft resulted largely from introductions from these two men.

P–E never experienced the same tight, centralized control or continuity of direction as its contemporaries. Both its founder and its managing director died comparatively young. Bryson, the first managing director, was killed in an air raid in 1941 while Lubbock the founder and chairman died in 1957. P–E was a natural focus of attention during the war drive when so many pioneering discoveries were made.

After the war the early patrons rallied round it, providing a spate of new contracts. More importantly, its different, less tightly controlled and arguably more aristocratic style of consultancy proved to be a powerful magnet for a distinguished band of young ex-officers who had matured very rapidly under wartime responsibilities. One of these was David Nicolson, a mechanical engineer who having served as a Lieutenant with the Royal Navy joined P–E in 1946 and became chairman in 1963. Sir David considers that 'One of P–E's big achievements just after the war, was to take on young men who had a basic qualification in either engineering or accountancy and supplement that by giving them scientific management training. This was something new and was a contribution. We always had the principle that if people stayed for a few years and worked for the company we wouldn't make it too hard for them if they wanted to move on.' Sir David himself moved on to take up a series of distinguished appointments, including the chairmanship of the British Airways Board.

Another distinguished young Royal Naval officer who joined P–E at about this time and later became managing director was Anthony Frodsham who moved on to take on the Director-Generalship of the Engineering Employers' Federation. The impact of the P–E philosophy can be seen by the fact that, by 1968, of 240 ex-employees, no fewer than 50 had become chairmen, managing directors, senior board members or divisional heads of well-known British companies. Today the annual dinner which P–E arranges for its old boys brings together an impressive gathering of senior industrialists who tend to regard themselves as members of a special club.

The idealist – Urwick

Of the founders of what later became the 'big four' management consultancy practices, Urwick, the idealist, was probably the least interested in the commercial aspects of running a consultancy. His own account of the disagreement with his founder partner, Leslie Orr, a Scottish production engineer who had been a sales manager with Bedaux, is not so much that it was about growth, as delegation – a subject on which Urwick held strong views.

Started in one room in Bloomsbury with two principals, two secretaries and no clients, Urwick Orr and Partners had four points of policy, none of which had much to do with the commercial aspects of the enterprise. These were: to develop a British approach to management consultancy; to exercise the highest possible professional standards of conduct; to develop a service across the whole spectrum of management (Urwick was more interested in administration and management than in production); and to obtain and maintain the goodwill of Organized Labour (a reaction to the hatred of the Bedaux unit). The first client, the owner of a laundry, is said to have arrived on the opening day. Another showing a very early interest was Sir Charles Renold of Renold Chains. Sir Charles, who later also became the first Chairman of the British Institute of Management, eventually became one of the first trustees of the company. Orr looked after the work measurement activities while Urwick operated in the clerical and managerial field. By 1939 and the outbreak of the Second World War the firm had about thirty consultants. Urwick's clerical work diminished since all the focus was on production and he went off to join the war, leaving Orr in charge.

Urwick's account of what happened when he returned is as follows:

> By 1945, when I returned to Urwick Orr & Partners Ltd (of which I was still Chairman), it was bursting at the seams. Under wartime restrictions we hadn't been allowed to add to our staff of consultants, but the demand was growing all the time. Orr couldn't delegate and he was furious with me when I tried to persuade him to do so.
>
> So I arranged for the rest of the Board to decide which of us they wanted to keep and they chose me. As I had warned them I would do, I simply split Great Britain into four areas, and gave them one each and said 'gallop, you bastards'. I merely kept recruiting, training and financial control in my own hands.
>
> We took big risks. Between 1945 and 1951 we expanded from 40 odd consultants to round about 150.
> [Letter to an MBA, published October 1969]

Urwick believed very strongly in both inspiration and the cultivation of the individual. His advice to young, newly qualified managers was to seek a purpose outside their own aims and ambitions and to stick to it – his own was to further the cause of management. He argued that such an objective gave both a yardstick and a buffer against human frailties. He also believed in people 'doing their own thing'.

> Do what you, and no one else, feel that you were meant to do, what to you is a sufficient reward for the labour and the sweat because it occupies your interest and intrigues your imagination. If you want to paint pictures and your father offers you the earth to make handbags, for heaven's sake paint pictures, however bloody bad they are. If you don't

you won't be a whole man . . . In your early jobs, go for the man every time. If you feel that an opportunity which opens up means working with an executive whom you can trust and like (above all with whom you can laugh) that's infinitely more important than title, salary or size of corporation.
[Letter to an MBA October 1969]

The 'big four'

By 1956, about three-quarters of all management consultancy work was channelled into these four firms: Inbucon, The P–E Consulting Group, Urwick Orr and Partners, and PA Management Consultants. Two had matured as businesses in the sense that second generation managers had taken over from the founders (although Urwick, as he had promised, kept a fatherly eye on things from afar by making regular visits from Australia for more than another thirty years). A third, P–E, was about to reach this stage. Only PA remained firmly in the hands of its originator.

The four firms presented a united front to the outside world. Their leaders participated, with varying degrees of enthusiasm, in the British Institute of Management. They combined more identifiably to protect collective standards, and to keep out outsiders whom they considered to be undesirable, through the Management Consultants Association. As a result of these activities they quickly became known as 'the big four'.

In private, however, there appears to have been little cross-fertilization between the companies or the consultants employed by them. Despite, or perhaps because of, their common origins, or perhaps because they were too busy operating in young companies in an exhilarating growth environment, there was no exchange of ideas or feeling of collective identity. Their leaders kept well apart from each other, and employees did not leave one consulting firm to join another.

Even wider cracks opened in the apparently united front in the differing views about whether the firms were in business or whether they were following some form of altruistic, non-commercial, professional path. None of the founders of the younger of the 'big four' wanted to be owners. Urwick handed control to Trustees in 1948. P–E's shares are held by pension and trust funds and the staff. Butten, who up to then had been the sole owner of PA, handed over to a trust fund set up for the benefit of past and present employees in 1958.

Commercial ambivalence

Absence of unity between the companies was seriously to weaken attempts to make a collective public case initially against the accountancy firms, and later, against quasi-Government contracts being given to foreign firms without an opportunity to tender for them. Ambivalence about the commercial aspects of their own businesses was forcibly ended by the abrupt downturn in trading conditions in the early 1970s; but not before it had seriously weakened some of the firms' abilities to meet the new, potentially long term investment-intensive challenges of new technology.

An outstanding exception, in terms of investment, is the centre for new product development set up by PA in the late 1960s. Patscentre (standing for PA Technology and Science Centre), set up as a subsidiary technical consultancy, was intended to give smaller and less technically advanced companies access to a team of highly skilled designers. In fact, large companies use it as well. One of the early clients was Plessey Telecommunications whose Edge Hill factory had been producing Strowger electro-mechanical telephone exchanges which were being phased out. Plessey approached Patscentre for an idea which could use outmoded production capacity to make something completely new. Patscentre's team of designers came up with a microprocessor-controlled pay telephone – a version of which is, at the time of writing, just being installed by British Telecom. The Patscentre concept was very much in keeping with the spirit of Butten's original charter in which research was regarded as complementary to operational work – the fees from the one going to feed the other.

Although strongly identified through Patscentre with the new technology from the outset, PA was as slow as its competitors to develop its potential in the operational sense. It was not until 1976 that it formed its Pactel (PA Computers and Telecommunications) division which provides the nuts and bolts consultancy service of skills and techniques in computer programming, software design and training.

Nevertheless PA's record in terms of growth has far outstripped that of its traditional competitors. With a turnover which in 1981 was approaching £54 million it provides about a quarter of all consultancy work originated in the United Kingdom.

But even the mighty PA's financial weight is not sufficient to hold the market dominance which was traditionally held by the big 'pure' consulting organizations. The last 20 years have seen considerable fragmentation and diversification in the structure of consulting activities. First, there has been the growth of the accounting groups' subsidiaries for whom computerization in company finance departments in the 1950s made a natural development path. Today, offshoots of four large accounting groups – Coopers & Lybrand Associates, Peat, Marwick, Mitchell & Co, Price Waterhouse Associates, and Deloitte Haskins and Sells – rank among the top ten on the management consultancy league table. Second has come competition from 'in house' groups formed by companies like Unilever, as well as the nationalized industries and quasi-governmental organizations like the industrial training boards, not to mention the business schools.

Emergence of the independents

A third and less predictable feature of today's management consultancy market has been the remarkable rise in the number of sole practitioners and small consultancy groups. Work carried out by these so-called 'independents' currently represents around a third of all British consultancy assignments in terms of fee income. Most of the independents have originated from the traditional 'big four' firms but some have also come from the accountancy firms' offshoots. They left for a variety of reasons and at different times. A trickle in the 1960s which became a flood in the mid-1970s is partly due to the recessionary conditions but also reflects a reaction to the bureaucracy which many consultants felt their profession had become and in which they felt straightjacketed. Some suffered from clashes of personality, inevitable in any groups which consist of strong-willed individuals. Others were frustrated by limited prospects for promotion. Many simply wanted to pursue a specialist activity in their own way.

There continues to be an interrelationship between the large firms and the independents both as a source of work and as a training ground. Nevertheless, if only in order to maintain their living standards, many of the new, small consultancy groups are becoming entrepreneurial businesses in their own right. As such they are cementing new relationships with clients and generating new work which in turn may feed back to the consultancy companies from which the small firms originated.

What is yet to become apparent is whether today's small consulting groups will remain small. Will they become absorbed into the large companies? Is their emergence a temporary phenomenon of recession? Will they grow into large organizations on their own account? Or will new methods of collaboration and co-operation evolve between consultants?

5
Criticisms and Comparisons

No serious complaint about a consultant's work has ever been submitted to the Institute of Management Consultants throughout its twenty year lifespan. This is not to suggest that all management consultants' work has always been impeccable. It is merely one indication of the absence of strong adverse feelings on the part of user organizations about the service they have received. When assignments have gone wrong, users, in the end, tend to feel that they are as much to blame as the consultant. Besides, consultants care passionately about their reputations and will normally do what they can to rectify mistakes on an individual basis.

There have been instances of consultants agreeing to waive or reduce their fees, or repeating the work free of charge when assignments have not been satisfactorily completed. It is normal practice for individual consultants to be pulled out and replaced if the client organization feels them to be insufficiently qualified, too young, or simply not to fit in.

Selling and publicizing its services so as to ensure a smooth flow of work has given the management consulting profession more teething troubles than any other aspect of its activities. Consultancy is best marketed on an individual basis. The problem is, first, in winning the right introductions, and second in convincing a businessman that a consultancy which is expert in one area can be equally expert in another so that he turns to the same firm who helped him, say, with his energy conservation programme for advice on computers.

Winning the right introductions is the most difficult of these processes. The fears and suspicions which are frequently associated with change tend to rub off on management consultants, making them unwelcome visitors. In the early days of multinationals, Americans whose attitude was to anticipate rather than react to change, consistently underestimated the strength of feeling against change in Europe. Nowhere was the difference between the two cultures in this respect highlighted more vividly than in the still infant management consulting profession.

George S. May

No sooner had the founders of the second generation of British consulting firms lived down the unwelcome associations with their Bedaux origins than the profession was rocked by the activities of another American firm, George S. May. The sales tactics used by May so upset that dignified and august body, the Institute of Chartered Accountants, that on 15 December 1960, it took the unprecedented step of issuing a warning naming the company and advising members not to recommend its services to clients. The explicit December warning followed a more discreetly worded salvo sent out by the I.C.A.'s Council a month earlier. This stated that members rendered themselves liable to disciplinary action if they accepted employment with organizations which advertised their services as consultants or advisers in management, costing methods, business organization and methods.

This, alone, would have been more than enough to subdue most British concerns but did not, apparently, daunt the Chicago-based George S. May. To the unholy glee of City onlookers, the company decided that attack was the best form of defence, and took the Establishment to the Courts. Not only did it start proceedings for libel against the I.C.A. – an unheard of step – but Anthony Lloyd, an accountant employed by May, and a member of the I.C.A., sought a court injunction to stop a disciplinary council hearing which alleged that he had been guilty of professional misconduct by being employed by an organization which offered its services by advertising. Lloyd, in turn, accused the Council of bias and said that it had prejudged the issue and the only available tribunal was the High Court.

The case, Lloyd *v*. The Institute of Chartered Accountants in England and Wales, came up before Mr Justice Wilberforce in October 1961. The Court heard that Mr Lloyd had been informed the preceding August that a complaint had been preferred against him by the I.C.A.'s Investigation Committee. The complaint alleged that, as a Fellow of the I.C.A., Mr Lloyd was guilty of 'acts or defaults discreditable to a member of the I.C.A., in that he was employed by an organization which, in its business as consultants or advisers in management costing and methods of business organization and administration, offered its services by advertising'. The court also heard that the company advertised its activities on a considerable scale.

In his summing up, the Judge said it must be accepted that the Council disapproved strongly of the activities of this particular company and also that it would 'not be realistic to assume otherwise than that relations between the I.C.A. and the company were hostile'. However, it seemed to him that it would be wrong to say that an employee could not be given a fair trial in respect of his individual professional conduct in any case where there was an attitude of hostility against his employer. There was no evidence of any particular bias against Mr Lloyd himself.

Accordingly he ruled against Lloyd and dismissed the motion against the I.C.A. with costs.

May's writ for libel limited public criticism about its activities. However it did nothing to allay the reservations that many businessmen have about management consultants even to this day. It was not the advertisement of the May Company that worried businessmen so much as what they considered were its high pressure sales tactics, such as its salesmen arriving unannounced and issuing dire forecasts about their future.

One of the effects of the May affair was to make British consultants even more diffident about marketing themselves than they had been before. Because of this, the established firms became yet more vulnerable to transatlantic competition from rivals which were becoming increasingly skilful in their use of publicity.

The Fawley agreement

A growing number of large and prestigious contracts were going to American consultancy firms at this time. One of the most famous of these involved economies in the use of manpower at the Fawley oil refinery.

The Esso oil refinery, added to existing facilities at Fawley near Southampton in the 1950s, was considered a model of good management practice. It was then the largest oil refinery in the Commonwealth with a throughput of crude oil ten times greater than the original refinery. Construction of it was a massive task involving over 5,000 construction workers, many of whom had to be housed in a special camp. When building was completed five months ahead of schedule, it made headline news and led to a paper being published by the British Institute of Management on the achievement in 1954. This stressed the combination of good planning with 'unusually smooth labour relations'.

There was naturally a good deal of attention focussed on Fawley when, three years later, the refinery's management negotiated a revolutionary productivity package with its unions. In return for a pay increase of about 40 per cent in five instalments spread over two years, the refinery management obtained trade union agreement to changes in demarcation rules and traditional use of craftsmen's mates which were hampering productivity. More significantly, the agreement successfully phased down overtime working which was, and still is, considered to be an undesirable feature of British labour management. In common with the rest of manufacturing industry, overtime working had been mounting steadily at Fawley during the 1950s. In 1952 it represented 5 per cent of total hours worked growing to 18 per cent by 1959 which, because of the premium rates paid, added around 32 per cent to the wages bill.

The agreement was conceived as a social experiment from the outset. A copy of the 'Blue Book' (named after the Esso management custom of placing larger documents and manuals between blue covers) detailing the agreement was sent to opinion formers including Allan Flanders, senior lecturer in industrial relations at Oxford University, shortly after the unions had received it.

Esso were interested in an independent enquiry being undertaken into their departure from conventional collective bargaining and offered Flanders every assistance in carrying out investigations. When he had obtained similar assurances of co-operation from the trade unions, he accepted the invitation and proceeded to write a detailed and very illuminating account of the proceedings from both sides of the negotiating table. (*The Fawley Productivity Agreements* by Allan Flanders: London: Faber and Faber, 1964.) It was recognized from the start that considerable changes in attitudes and working practices were needed by both unions and management for the negotiations to succeed. Even so, there were many periods of near breakdown during two years of exhaustive formal and informal planning and discussion.

The Fawley agreement still stands not only as a landmark in industrial relations history but also provides a classic illustration of management consultancy in operation. Two firms were invited to tender for the work. One was the American consulting firm of Emerson's which had been mentioned by the contract director of the plant on the strength of what he had heard about their work in American refineries. The other was a British firm which had been selected for its knowledge of labour relations and some familiarity with the oil industry.

The two firms carried out provisional surveys and submitted their reports. In Flanders' view, the most that the British firm seemed likely to offer was an incentive bonus scheme on a productivity basis and this approach was regarded as both outmoded and inappropriate for the industry. On the other hand, the breadth of the Emerson report which 'showed that they were management consultants in the fullest sense, not merely method study engineers' told in their favour as did their greater refining experience.

Moreover, the very fact that the company was American also carried weight. In the words of one of the members of management concerned with the decision, 'This to my mind had a strange advantage. It meant that they were certainly not biassed and that they could plead ignorance of trade unions. And because of our history of often using Americans as start-up advisers, our people were used to seeing them around, so that they were less likely to cause friction than having a British consultant.'

Flanders recounts that not everybody shared this view. In fact, the idea of introducing consultants of any nationality was not greeted with any enthusiasm, particularly by the men who were running the maintenance and construction department who saw it as a questioning of their own abilities. The assistant superintendent of that department who had difficulty in persuading his colleagues made the point as follows:

> I think the grounds were really this question of pride in doing it oneself. This was in fact an admission in some people's eyes that we had not succeeded in doing certain things, that we had to bring in somebody else. Their attitude was – give us a chance of doing it and we will show you that we can. Up to now we have never been given the chance. Of course the

answer to that is that whilst trying to do it ourselves we would never be given the chance; we would never succeed in getting the confidence at all levels to put this through.

Of course, this was precisely the reason why external consultants were required. They could mediate between both unions and management because they did not belong to either. They were not concerned with traditional methods or internal politics and had no axe to grind.

Two of Emerson's consultants appeared at Fawley in February 1958. The then senior man was 'the more orthodox type of consultant, meticulous and exact, relying primarily on the various techniques of job analysis and work study and supported by his knowledge of oil refinery organization in the United States', according to Flanders' description. His colleague had a different background and attitude towards the work. Comments about him made by members of Fawley management were that 'he was the deep thinker', and, most important, that 'he was very good at getting other people to think'. Apart from having broad cultural as well as intellectual interests, he had come into consultancy after university studies in the social sciences. He is also described as a man with 'firm convictions and abundant self-confidence'.

Discounting any prejudice which could have arisen from Flanders' own background, the contrast between the two is of interest in illustrating very different styles of consultancy which are still in evidence today, more than twenty years later.

At first, in the words of one of the negotiating group, the consultants 'were very brash about the whole thing . . . and made all sorts of suggestions separately and jointly. Such ideas as cutting back of wages to show we mean business. Why don't you just stop having mates?' Fortunately, perhaps, at this stage they were not talking to shop stewards or the men on the shop floor. It had been clearly understood that they would first direct their main attention to the shortcomings of managerial organization in the maintenance and construction department. Their recommendations on this score were drawn up and a new management structure came into effect at the end of September 1958.

The pros and cons of the reorganization were thoroughly aired at various consultative committee meetings. At these the consultants' position and role was once again argued, this time by the trade unions. Remarks by the main spokesman for the union councillors illustrate the reaction; he said 'he was not against efficiency etc. and he felt that the works councillors had told the consultants a lot more than they could tell the councillors. Nevertheless, it seemed rather peculiar to bring these consultants all the way from the States; it seemed that ideas were not taken sufficient notice of here and this seemed to be the only way to get action taken.'

A representative for management replied that:

> The basic reason why they were here was not because everyone here was not full of ideas, but because the refinery had grown from employing 1,000 to nearly 3,500 in six years, and as everyone had been getting on with the job there had been no time to sit back and think about things. It was thought much better for someone outside the refinery to take a look at the position as they could do it more objectively. Problems tend not to be recognized by people who had lived with them for six years. The consultants were American purely because they were the best we could get.

However, although it had taken about nine months, the consultants were, in fact, becoming accepted and, moreover, had become involved in the situation. About this time they issued the first of two memoranda which were to have a profound effect on events. The first criticized the management of the refinery for having 'reacted rather than acted' to the consultative process and for not anticipating the strength of the shop stewards' position.

'Because the stewards' position was not anticipated, management was caught off guard,' it said. It also urged management to take a more active part and show more initiative at Works Council meetings.

That memorandum was followed by a second, even more pungently expressed, document which suggested the main lines on which a strong managerial initiative could be taken. Flanders describes this as forming the 'springboard' of the final agreement since it compelled a re-examination of what were previously fixed ideas about wages and overtime policy. The consultants' case for a low overtime and high wage policy was a decided break with the prevailing thought and practice. It had come to be accepted first, that wages at Fawley should be roughly equivalent to those paid by other employers in the area, and second, that overtime was inevitable for both technical reasons and to satisfy the workers. In contrast, the consultants' view was that overtime could be got rid of without putting very much in its place. American refineries were running without it, why not Fawley?

The initial reaction was that they were asking for the impossible. The superintendent of the department said that even though the suggestions 'gave everybody at long last a glimmer of light about how something could be done, it all seemed hopelessly idealistic and utterly out of touch with our situation and the inevitable first reactions to it were ones of extreme cynicism and "why doesn't he go home?" '

Even though the ideas were considered to be impractical, discussions about them continued for more than six months with meetings once or twice a week. By the middle of September 1959, about ten months after the second memorandum was compiled, some embryonic ideas were beginning to germinate as to how they could be made to work.

The consultants had by now moved on to another department, leaving the Superintendent and his colleagues to devise a plan which later became an extended system of shifts as a method of replacing systematic overtime.

The consultants' role in the technical aspects of drawing up the proposals was largely as a catalyst. They were seen as playing a much more direct part than they in fact did in influencing a change of attitudes by both management and unions without which the changes could not have been introduced. Towards the end of 1959, Flanders recounts, the consultants deliberately set out to prepare the minds of the men and their union representatives for a change just as they had previously tackled management.

The difference was that among management they had enjoyed a standing that supported their authority; among the stewards this was more likely to arouse suspicion and distrust. Being Americans proved an advantage. It allowed them to act as interested enquirers into British trade union practices which indeed they were. That they should want to query assumptions that were alien to their own culture was considered natural enough. By the latter part of 1959 the consultants were involved in regular and at times almost daily discussions with some of the senior stewards, in which the ideas behind the Blue Book were introduced and argued about in terms of justification, long before there was a money offer and the formal negotiations started.

Having thus described the consultants' activities in fairly glowing terms, Flanders then rather denigrates their contribution in his conclusion:

> The value of consultants per se was simply that of a catalytic agent; their independent status made it possible to speed up the process of change in managerial attitudes and beliefs. How they would influence labour relations and how useful and constructive their influence would be, could not have been foreseen. The choice of the particular firm was based largely on a hunch that they would bring a fresh mind and the right kind of experience into the situation. Neither their preliminary report nor what they had accomplished in the American refineries provided even the glimmerings of an anticipation of the Blue Book. That one of the consultants turned out to be the man he was, and that he did in fact contribute a great deal to the growth of managerial initiative in labour relations, was purely fortuitous.

The Fawley agreement has gone down as a momentous pioneering step in the history of industrial relations. Although, with hindsight, it could be argued that it raised as many problems as it removed, at the time it was given a largely unqualified welcome. Many companies seized on productivity agreements as the answer to problems arising from poor manning methods without appreciating the complexities and consequences of the changes. A spate of carelessly applied imitations was unleashed with the backing of a Government which, at the time, regarded increased productivity as a cure for all economic ills. During the periods of pay restraint which followed, productivity bargaining became the simplest way of bypassing the norm.

Stampede for productivity

There was a rush for job evaluation and work measurement schemes as not just production workers, but stockroom and office personnel as well climbed on to the bandwagon. A multitude of productivity and efficiency agreements covering over 6 million workers had sprouted by the end of the decade. Wages escalated so that in 1969, despite the stated 'norm' of an increase of 3 per cent, the actual increase in earnings amounted to nearly 9 per cent. Workers who had previously co-operated freely and willingly on improvements in working methods began to see that they possessed a saleable commodity. Not all groups of workers were able to improve their output to the same extent, which distorted the difference in earnings between different groups, significantly weakened the position of first line managers, and resulted in unfairness of reward for equal effort.

Many of the disadvantages are only just becoming generally recognized. For behind the schemes lay an all-out drive for increased output which obscured many of the problems. For management consultants too, the climate was one of apparently boundless growth. The British firms, however, were becoming increasingly aware that many of the plum assignments involving top level organizational work in prestigious organizations were going to their American rivals, and to one company in particular – McKinsey.

McKinsey Company

The McKinsey consulting company set up an office in London in 1959 specifically to deal with organization and boardroom management. It had no heritage of work study and Hugh Parker, the suave, quietly spoken managing director was a far remove from the stereotyped 'efficiency expert' with which British companies had become identified.

Born into a middle class Boston family in 1919, Parker's father retired from the family business and moved the family to Munich when he was nine. 'My parents had the then fairly unorthodox idea that my two brothers and I should learn a couple of foreign languages,' he told the editor of *Atlantic*, the magazine of the American Chamber of Commerce. After returning to the United States at the age of 14 he started travelling again, this time on an ESU exchange scholarship from the Tabor academy in Massachusetts to Felsted School in Essex. At Tabor he showed proficiency at rowing which he continued at Trinity Hall Cambridge – studying economics and engineering – and winning the Boat Race in 1939. 'That was a wonderful moment, it was almost like being Royalty. In those days the Boat Race got a great deal of press coverage,' Parker said. Not only did his early experiences give him first hand knowledge of how the British media worked, it also gave him the introduction to the inner Establishment circles which so many of his rivals lacked.

After the war and a spell with General Electric and in India with the Ludlow Manufacturing Company where he became interested in scientific management, he joined McKinsey & Company in 1951 as a junior consultant in New York. Work for the Royal Dutch Shell group took him first to Venezuela and then to London. As the Shell project reached completion, McKinsey's top management decided that London should be the base of the firm's first overseas office, and Parker was appointed the first managing director.

A comparatively small number of consultants were recruited – in 1968 McKinsey had about 74 as against PA Management Consultants' total of over 400 – but they were encouraged to consider themselves an intellectual elite. Sir Roger Falk who was at the P–E Consulting Group at the time confesses to being an admirer of McKinsey in this respect: 'When the big British four were growing fast, they tended to become more and more specialised whereas Hugh Parker and Co. were marvellous in the sense that they always went for cultivated and broadly based people.' McKinsey consultants were also paid well and encouraged to move on into industry after a few years.

Whether it was Parker's introductions, his high calibre staff, or a ruthless approach to bureaucracy (it is said that McKinsey's recommendations cut down Shell's staff by a third) or a combination of all of these, the company became fashionable. Subtle use of public relations certainly played an important part. So did the fact that the firm was American. It was not necessarily thought that Americans were better but just, as one chairman remarked at the time, 'They won't take it from anyone else.'

Unlike some of its rivals, McKinsey maintains no large Public Relations department. Instead, discreetly worded announcements about their appointment were sent out by client organizations to newspaper city editors. Instead of trying to conceal the use of management consultants, institutions were starting to become rather proud of their initiative in this respect.

British riposte

British management consultants looked on enviously as a succession of prestigious names were publicly chalked up against that of McKinsey. Shell was followed by ICI and Dunlop; the Post Office, by the BBC, British Rail, British Steel, and the Gas Council. British consultants became increasingly restive. Their traditional reticence snapped when on 28 October 1968 the Bank of England issued an announcement to the press saying, 'Preliminary discussions are taking place with McKinsey with a view to their undertaking a study of the organisation and methods of the work of the Bank.' There was, by now, a high degree of public interest in business generally and particular curiosity about the workings of management consultants. City pages of newspapers had recently been expanded and the announcement was given extensive coverage. 'Bank of England working to be examined by McKinsey' was the restrained headline given by the *Financial Times* the following day but 'The Axe Man Cometh to the Bank of England', screamed the *Sheffield Star* while the *Daily Express* shouted 'Slide Rule Men from US Called To The Bank'.

What upset the British companies was that they had not been given a chance to tender for the contract. The first they knew of the assignment was what they read about it in the newspapers. Anthony Frodsham of the P–E Consulting Group, then chairman of the Management Consultants Association which represented 19 of the established firms, decided to retaliate. He immediately sought a meeting with Sir Leslie O'Brien, Governor of the Bank of England. This was followed by a letter to the Prime Minister and a question in the House of Commons.

Questions in the House

Protests from MPs of all parties took up much of the Prime Minister's Question Time on 19 November. Mr Harold Wilson, the Prime Minister, expressed doubts about the Bank of England's decision during the discussion. He said he thought that British firms of consultants had the double advantage of knowing the terrain better than American firms and of generally charging lower fees. On 27 November, came a full blooded Parliamentary debate on the question of public bodies and United States management consultants, at which MPs again were generally sympathetic about the contribution of consultants in general. *Hansard*'s record of the debate shows that a thorough airing was given to the British consultants' complaint that their status overseas had been damaged because the Bank of England had chosen an American company.

A blow by blow account of progress was given in the press. Photographs began to replace the cartoon drawings of Chicago-style gangster figures carrying violin cases with captions like 'They say they're the American efficiency consultants' or 'How do I know you're not Al Capone?'. For the first time the public could see for themselves that what had hitherto been regarded as rather sinister shadows were as human as any other businessmen. A smiling Frodsham accompanied by a beaming Tony Howitt, president of the Institute of Management Consultants, appeared in *The Times* after their meeting with Sir Leslie O'Brien – where they were received with sympathy but given no apology. Even so, the objective, which was that a strong expression of views would prevent a repetition of a Government-linked organization picking a consultant without putting the assignment out for tender, had been reached.

However, as the publicity bandwagon continued to roll, exceeding all expectations ('I think we rather overdid it,' Frodsham said later) it became apparent that there was a split in the established consultants' own ranks. One eminent practitioner even rang up Hugh Parker to say how ashamed he was of the way his fellow consultants had been carrying on. Others made more muted complaints.

Frodsham had been trying to convince his colleagues in the Management Consultants Association for some time that, like McKinsey, they should be more open about their clients from the beginning: 'Just like an engagement', he said, 'the first day is the happiest and that is when the match should be announced.' Others vehemently disagreed. 'How stupid can a client get when publicity starts at the beginning of a job?', commented one.

Buy British

Despite a valiant attempt to present a united front, it became cruelly obvious that, having reached the very centre of the public stage, management consultants were uncertain about their collective role there. In many ways their collective reactions at this time mirrored the insecurities which managers were to display a few years later. In any event, the 'Buy British' furore over the McKinsey and Bank of England affair, although considered something of a storm in a teacup at the time, in fact marked the end of a development stage. Management consultants were no longer hidden by mystique. From now on they were required, increasingly, to work alongside their clients both metaphorically and physically, to explain their methods and to come up with tangible results.

The McKinsey affair also marked an end to the tendency for the United States to be regarded as the mother and therefore automatically better in all matters relating to management. An umbilical cord had been severed by the public declaration that British consultants could stand on equal terms with their transatlantic counterparts.

'We have got to have more faith in our British abilities, most of the specialisation claimed by foreigners exists here,' Frodsham thundered. What really rankled was the unfairness of the assumption that no British consultancy had suitable experience. When challenged on its choice, the Bank of England's private response is said to have been, 'We didn't know you did that sort of thing.' Although production work accounted for over 40 per cent of the established firms' fees, they had also carried out some major organization projects – for companies like Standard Telephones and Cables and Guest Keen and Nettlefolds. Ironically, British consultancies were carrying out organizational assignments for the Swiss Post Office and the New Zealand Broadcasting Commission at the same time as McKinsey had been chosen by their United Kingdom counterparts.

'What is so bad and so wrong,' commented Frodsham, 'is that British firms are patently seen not to have been consulted. It gives the whole world the impression that only American firms are competent to handle this sort of job.' He added, 'It's not sour grapes; we just haven't been given a chance.'

Muted complaints

Many older consultants express nostalgic regrets about the shift into specialization and the stress on tangible benefits which have been features of the last ten years. Nevertheless, together with consultants' own efforts to sharpen their expertise, it effectively dampened the many unspecific and often snide criticisms about management consultants which were rife in the 1960s.

Probably the last salvo of this type was fired by Robert Townsend, former chairman of the Avis Rent-a-Car Corporation, in his book *Up the Organization* (London: Michael Joseph, 1970). 'The effective ones are the one-man shows. The institutional ones are disastrous,' Townsend wrote about management consultants. 'They waste time, cost money, demoralize and distract your best people, and don't solve problems. They are people who borrow your watch to tell you what time it is and then walk off with it.'

Although flippant, Townsend's remark summarizes many of the concerns expressed more specifically to Philip W. Shay and recorded by the American Association of Consulting Management Engineers (*How to get the Best Results from Management Consultants*, 1974). 'We have the impression they wanted us as clients only to say that we had been their client,' said one chief executive. 'They picked the brains of our own people and rehashed these opinions in a fancy report. They didn't tell us anything we didn't know already. They didn't contribute any new approach,' said another. 'They want to come in and install pre-packaged solutions to our problems. They are not aware, and don't make themselves aware of our particular needs,' said a third.

Similar complaints have been made by dissatisfied British clients. The General Secretary of a voluntary association which employed three management consultants for about four weeks in 1969 made the following comments:

> I think they probably do a good job for a business concern but what they did for us could have been got out of a textbook . . . They produced a beautifully presented report with some useful suggestions about equipment . . . but they did not really get to the nub of the problem and tell us how to achieve it. The principal recommendation was that two entirely new posts be created . . . which were to 'supervise' several departments each. These already worked direct to sub-committees with voluntary chairmen and through them to the Executive . . . The consultants seem to have entirely missed the point.
>
> I think they can be useful in recommending methods of work at the office work level, but they have no comprehension of how a voluntary organization worked and the rather delicate relationship between the membership . . . from whom support, and in the long run cash comes; and the other delicate relationship between committee members elected by the membership and the staff whom they employ.

These, and similar complaints, have lessened as management consultancy has matured, slimmed down, and sharpened up its expertise. At the end of the day, as the absence of formal complaints made to the professional Institute indicates, the onus falls back on managers to select and control their advisers and to use them wisely if the results are to be beneficial.

6
The Quest for Professional Recognition

Is management consultancy a profession or is it a business? This is still a contentious question among the ranks of consultants themselves, as well as a matter of debate amongst the users of their services. Without becoming immersed in the finer nuances of the definition of a profession, however, it seems clear that, to survive, management consultants must adhere to the same business ethics as, for instance, accountants, engineers or lawyers.

In order to work properly they must enjoy an intimate relationship with their clients under which they can be taken completely into confidence. On a more pragmatic level, more than 3,000 management consultants have sufficiently high regard for their own status to belong to an Institute of Management Consultants which has the avowed aim of making 'the profession of management consultants recognised, respected and accepted'.

Through this Institute, consultants are moving steadily towards full public recognition although they acknowledge that the process is still far from complete. The first steps were taken in the early 1960s when management consultancy was showing all the signs of the boom conditions which materialized later in the decade. The final destination, which could be the granting of a Royal Charter with all that it implies, is unlikely to be reached for another decade or more.

As so often happens, the impetus to start management consultants along the route to winning professional recognition came from a combination of external conditions and a handful of dedicated people. In the early 1960s, the established British consultancy firms were starting to meet fierce competition not only from more glamorous American counterparts but also from a variety of home-grown rivals including accountants, who were fast spreading their wings far outside their traditional spheres.

The new arrivals added to the general confusion amongst clients and potential clients about the breadth of services which management consultants could be expected to provide. As one contemporary participant says, 'the attitude then was very much that of "who are these chaps and are they any good?"' The Bank of England was by no means unique in its perceptions (described in the preceding chapter). But while the prewar stereotype of time-and-motion merchants may have hit the consultancy companies in their balance sheets, individual practitioners suffered more from it in their day to day work.

By now, consultants' services were in demand in the boardroom where trust in the consultant is vital, as well as on the factory floor where results are more quickly visible and measurable. But despite the significant contributions being made to national economic restructuring, management consultants became the butt of popular humorists. Geoffrey Buss, the 1981–82 President of the Institute of Management Consultants who entered management consultancy in the 1950s, reflects the experiences of many of his generation when he recalls that on social occasions 'people more often than not responded with a funny remark when you told them you were a consultant – this still happens but only occasionally.'

Despite the existence of a register of consultants operated by the British Institute of Management and the efforts of the Management Consultants Association, there was still confusion about the standards of service which could be expected. The register had been set up by the British Institute of Management in the late 1940s in order 'to sort out the sheep from the goats', as one consultant involved describes it. Like the Management Consulting Services Information Bureau which superseded it in 1965, however, the register's primary function was to help users rather than consultants. In addition, the first registration committee, at least, regarded the register as a temporary measure pending the establishment of a professional institute.

Formation of MCA

The Management Consultants Association formed in 1956 by the four largest British consultancy companies: PA, P–E, Urwick Orr and Inbucon was a sort of hybrid. Its founder companies, all of which remained on the British Institute of Management's register, appeared to look to cooperation mainly for promotional reasons. The Association did not attempt to set itself up to examine individuals or provide them with qualifications.

It was widely felt that something more was needed to enhance the status of both individuals and their work. Envious glances were cast then, as now, at the privileged legal status as well as to the public recognition accorded to accountants and lawyers. In addition, and perhaps more importantly, established practitioners felt that a mechanism was needed to safeguard future standards by providing a qualification which could be recognized by clients.

Pressure for an institution, separate from the Management Consultants Association and which would comprise individuals rather than companies, came from several quarters. First there was a groundswell of criticism from outside the Association, particularly from accountants, that it had given itself terms of reference which were too narrow for the future needs of an activity showing all the signs of rapid growth. At that time the Board of Trade estimated that there were about 200 firms of consultants operating in the United Kingdom. While the Management Consultants Association's members accounted for about three-quarters of business by turnover, it contained only five companies in membership.

Second, there was pressure from a group of dissidents from within the Association itself. Led by Jim Sandford Smith who later became the founder president of the Institute of Management Consultants, this group had become increasingly unhappy about what it considered an unacceptable conflict of interest between the activities of a trade association and those of a professional organization.

Individuals combine

The catalyst which brought the pressures to a head was a proposal made by two young accountants in July 1961 to set up their own Institute independently. The Association's council members, some of whom had been approached by the accountants, took the threat seriously. They sought legal advice to establish that the Association had no legal claim over the name Institute of Management Consultants and formed a subcommittee consisting of Jim Sandford

Smith and William Coutts Donald to submit proposals for the Association itself to sponsor an Institute.

Their alarm is reflected in the following extract from a letter written by a member of the council to Harry Piper, the Association's secretary:

Mr — is a young and apparently earnest man who is a chartered accountant and practising as a management consultant in matters concerning office procedures and accounting. He brought with him a Mr — of similar age (early 30s) who says that he practises as a consultant with Mr — on a part-time basis but is also connected with an organisation for the supply of office equipment.

While Mr —'s proposal for the formation of an Institute of Management Consultants is clothed in altruistic motives, it is fairly clear that he is anxious to promote his own interests. He said that there were obvious difficulties in negotiations with prospective clients when he was unable to point to any qualification which marked him as a management consultant. He also said he had had conversations with — and Partners (a highly respected company which was not a member of the Association) who shared his view.

Many of the proposals which he had to make in connection with the Institute of Management Consultants could well be covered and in many cases, are already covered by M.C.A. . . . There is danger in the situation insofar as M.C.A. can be embarrassed by the creation of such an Institute if M.C.A. itself were not responsible for the formation. It is conceivable (although it might not be envisaged at the present by Mr —) that he could obtain support from the Institute of Chartered Accountants in their attempt to curb the professional code of conduct of M.C.A.

If M.C.A. does not create an Institute of Management Consultants there is considerable risk that someone else may succeed in doing so. I think we should give the matter consideration.

To this letter, Harry Piper added a footnote when submitting it to the Association's Council, to the effect that he had consulted solicitors on how a rival association could be prevented from using the name 'Institute of Management Consultants'. In this he said, 'It might be possible, if we so wish, to change our name on incorporation to "The Institute of Management Consultants" but it is by no means certain that the Board of Trade would agree to this as our membership is for businesses and not individuals.'

A momentous Extraordinary Meeting was held by the Management Consultants Association's Council on Wednesday, 1 November 1961. At this, it unanimously agreed on two fundamental changes. First that the Association should sponsor an independent Institute of Management Consultants to deal with matters affecting management consulting as a profession. Second that while the Association should continue to pursue its present aims, it should do so as a trade association. This ended a long internal wrangle within the Association as to whether or not it was a trade body and freed the many individuals within member companies and outside who wanted to work towards full recognition as a profession.

A five man steering group was formed to hammer out the details of the new Institute. This consisted, in addition to Jim Sandford Smith (of Harold Whitehead and Partners) and William Coutts Donald (of Urwick Orr and Partners), of J. A. Bishop (of Inbucon), T. P. Bowman (of PA) and A. F. Frodsham (of P–E). Later Oliver Roskill (of O. W. Roskill Industrial Consultants) was invited to join.

The steering group met immediately after the Association's Council announced its decision when it unanimously elected Jim Sandford Smith the first president of the Institute and Harry Piper as the first secretary. It held a longer meeting a fortnight later and met again at monthly intervals for the next twelve months.

Anthony Frodsham recalls that the atmosphere was immediately much freer at Institute meetings than when the same people met as representatives of their companies. 'You must remember that the chief executives of the management consulting companies at that time barely knew each other. Even though they had common origins, a whole generation or more had passed. That was a period of great postwar expansion. We thought we had the world at our feet and that our rivals were devils. We couldn't concede that a competitor knew anything.'

Frodsham explains that shortly before the Management Consultants Association had been founded, he went to a meeting of the Comité International de l'Organisation Scientifique in Paris, where the French introduced the British management consultants to each other because they wanted to form an international management consultancy organization. In fact the British M.C.A. became a founder member of the Fédération Européenne des Associations de Conseils en Organisation which was formed in 1960.

'That was the first time I met counterparts such as E. B. Butten [of PA] and Lyndall Urwick [Urwick Orr and Partners]' continues Frodsham. 'As a member of both the Association and the Institute, I found that we were enormously suspicious of each other on the

Association, but the same people felt much more at ease once we started the Institute.'

Ethics and standards

In addition to drawing up a detailed memorandum outlining the requirements needed for professional status, Sandford Smith and Coutts Donald had also produced a fully fledged draft scheme stating how this could be achieved. In this they said, 'No true profession can be based on the qualifying of firms – it must be based on qualifying the individual. Many new professions have been accepted within the last 50 years, all have followed the principles of the professions which first gained public recognition as such – medicine and the law, engineering and accountancy.'

Four elements were identified in this original memorandum as established essential elements for a profession:

1. A body of knowledge.
   There must be a recognized body of knowledge in which a practitioner must be proficient.
2. Training.
   A period of studentship or service during which the body of knowledge will be studied, and experience of the profession gained by the new entrant.
3. Qualifying examinations.
   The passing of one or a series of examinations by which the governing body of the profession can be satisfied that after the period of service, the individual has acquired adequate knowledge and experience to be accepted into the profession.
4. Maintenance of professional standards.
   The establishment of a professional code and of rules of conduct, and the setting up of a disciplinary body of the profession with power to disqualify any member failing to maintain professional standards.

These elements have been more succinctly described as a 'concern with the knowledge, conduct and competence of individual members'. Roger Falk who at the time was president of the

Institute once listed (a) a satisfactory registration procedure; (b) a system of qualifying examinations; (c) a professional training establishment; and (d) legal protection of the term 'management consultant' in the institutions and procedures which he considered necessary to make management consulting a true profession and to put it on a similar basis to the larger established professions.

The emphasis and description may vary, but broadly speaking the original blueprint for the Institute contained all the ingredients commonly agreed to be necessary for professional recognition. Even so (as is always the way when management consultants meet together) every point had to be debated by the steering committee from first principles. Some of the discussions which started then have continued ever since.

Business or profession?

One of the first divisions of opinion was about defining a profession and whether management consultants should model themselves on the older established professions or should follow a new route – or whether indeed they should consider themselves primarily as businessmen operating in a highly competitive environment. From this has stemmed ambivalence to such questions as entry by examination and attitudes to promotion by advertisement.

Nevertheless, despite the long and argumentative debates, tangible progress was made. By December 1961, soundings had been taken from a variety of related organizations. The results were very mixed.

The Institute of Chartered Accountants welcomed the arrival of the infant Institute from the start. Attitudes of other organizations ranged from indifference to hostility.

Early minutes record that initial reaction by the engineering institutions was one of disapproval. Two principal points were argued. The first was that there were no grounds for the formation: what was intended could be done by the Management Consultants Association; the second, that it was inappropriate for the Association to set up a qualifying body. The engineering institutions also maintained that there were no appropriate grounds for a 'Professional Institute' and that there were no means of establishing a proper qualification. All these arguments were reflected at the time and have been since within the consultants' own ranks.

Opposition from the British Institute of Management stemmed from a different and more self-interested source. The BIM had recently been attempting to promote its own register more extensively. It had undertaken a short advertising campaign in August 1959 and held a one-day conference of registered consultants in May 1960. Understandably, its reaction to the fledgling Institute at this time was not one of joyous welcome.

At any rate the Institute steering group's minutes record, 'From our discussions it is likely that the BIM will be antagonistic – almost violently so – on the grounds that they may lose subscriptions from members and that the present levies paid by consulting firms to be put on the BIM Register of Consultants will be discontinued.' Indeed, from the outset in its initial calculations of subscriptions, the steering group had included the likelihood that new Institute members, i.e. those from companies outside membership of the Management Consultants Association, would come from consultants registered with the BIM.

One of the advantages which greatly assisted a speedy start to the Institute was that it was able to share office premises (a situation which continues to this day) with the Association. In addition, Harry Piper, who had been Secretary to the Association and became the Institute's first Secretary, assisted greatly in compiling the early documentation and setting up administrative procedures. It was he who prepared the first draft Body of Knowledge and Experience of which, while the detail has been revised, the structure still remains.

By the beginning of 1962, work had started on preparing the Memorandum and Articles of Association for the new Institute. A number of lunches were held to explain the aims of the embryo new profession to other organizations. On 7 May 1962 at the Belfrey Club of Belgrave Square, Jim Sandford Smith met Sir Norman Kipping of the Federation of British Industry, Sir George Pollock of the Employers Federation, and Sir Charles Norriss of the National Productivity Council. Other lunches included the president and secretary of the Institute of Cost and Works Accountants.

Nevertheless, behind the scenes, important differences still remained despite the apparent harmony in public. On 21 June 1962, the steering group decided that the Institute 'should not be publicly launched until some important matters of principle had been decided'.

Definitions

One of these was the question of membership. Who should be admitted and who should not? Questions raised by Oliver Roskill in a paper submitted early in 1962 recurred again and again. Roskill maintained that there was a significant difference between an industrial and a management consultant. Should membership be confined to management consultants or should consultants like his own firm which specialized in specific areas be eligible?

On the matter of exams, Roskill wrote,

> The proposed body seeks to become a qualifying body, and, indeed unless it can in due course establish qualifications by a combination of examination and practical experience it seems likely to fail in its main (and agreed) aim of improving standards in the profession. Should not the Steering Committee tackle the problem of the Syllabus and if it did would it be possible to reach agreement? . . .
>
> Is there a body of knowledge on which the work of a management and industrial consultant is based and in which candidates be examined? Are there to be any restrictions on candidates resulting from the firms by which they are employed for example firms which are subsidiaries of or associated with foreign consulting organizations? If there are to be no restrictions, the problems of definition of management and industrial consultants mentioned in paragraph two will arise again on a bigger scale. What is the attitude to employees of firms in other professions who are increasingly expanding into the fields hitherto regarded as those of management and industrial consultants?

In addition to mentioning accountants and consulting engineers in this category, Roskill also singled out a number of others. These included employee selection and appointment firms 'who do some consulting work on personnel matters and more recently, I understand, in other fields as well,' market research firms and companies specializing in works layout who describe their activities as 'co-ordinated consultancy'.

Incorporation

Despite all the doubts and arguments, a sufficient consensus was reached by the steering committee for it to carry on with the steps to gain incorporation. On 17 October 1962, the new Institute was duly granted its certificate under the Companies Act. The first stage had begun.

The Institute was now a tangible entity. It had a Certificate of Incorporation and a Memorandum and Articles of Association. It had a Council, a Secretary and premises. However, in deference to the many, legitimate, arguments put up by dissidents from amongst the steering committee as well as amongst management consultants generally, the launch was a low key affair. The foundations had to be allowed to settle.

Professional recognition was at all times regarded as a multi-staged process. It was recognized from the beginning that transitions could only be achieved gradually and in phases although it was not, perhaps, fully acknowledged how lengthy some of the phases might be. From the start it was acknowledged that consultants had to obtain recognition as professionals in their own eyes before they could even begin to influence Government (and so begin the procedure of obtaining a Royal Charter).

Between incorporation and acceptance of the first applications for membership in April 1964, many more discussions and debates were held on the Body of Knowledge, the Code of Professional Conduct and the conditions of membership. However by early 1964 the Institute was open for business and the first 520 members enrolled.

The start of the second phase, once the foundations had settled and the first bricks were laid, was marked by the formal granting of a Coat of Arms in 1965 by the College of Arms. This elaborate crest which can be seen on the Institute's notepaper sits above the motto 'knowledge and progress'. It nostalgically reflects the confidence and ebullience amongst businessmen of the day, with its cogwheel set within a flaming sun to signify industry and business within the overall approach and embracing nature of consultants' work.

Financial independence

The Institute, of course, started without funds. It was financed in its early years by over £6,000 given by Management Consultants Association firms. A prime requirement at this time was to win recognition amongst consultants themselves – a measure of which is the number of subscriptions. A landmark was reached by April 1967 when Anthony Frodsham in his President's Address was able to report that the Institute had paid its way in the previous year with a small sum carried forward. The figures showed that membership stood at 1,350 of whom 1,080 were full members; 270 were associates; and about 60 worked abroad. Significantly, nearly 30 per cent of members were from non-Association member firms. With independence both financially and in composition of membership well in sight, the Institute was now set to assume its own independent identity.

Progress was, however, to be disappointingly slow. The next landmark, the introduction of entry by examination, was not to come for another thirteen years. The delay was partly because consultancy itself had hit a crisis period. All voluntary organizations depend on the collective spare energy of their members. At this time consultants had very little energy to spare from the day-to-day running of their operations.

Changes within professional groups are always fraught with intellectual debates and disputes. By now the Institute was a sizeable organization. The principles and structures of its founders had to be disseminated and debated amongst the newly recruited rank and file members. The policy-making Council of the Institute met (and still meets) only four times a year and there were endless opportunities for delay and stalling mechanisms by members who were not fully in accord with the original basic aims.

A qualifying examination procedure had been identified as a prerequisite of the Institute from its inception. It was seen not only as desirable in its own right, but also as an essential step towards obtaining a Royal Charter which, in turn, was seen by some as the most effective method of winning official recognition of professional status. Advice sought by the original Steering Group under Jim Sandford Smith had established that, in order to gain Government recognition, one of the requirements was that the majority of members should have been admitted by examination. Without such recognition, no Royal Charter would be forthcoming.

But while the principles had been accepted early on in the Institute's life there were horrific problems in implementing such a procedure. One of the big difficulties with setting examinations for management consultants is that their work spans such a wide field. Other professions have knowledge which is special to themselves. Some of that knowledge relating to management consultants is shared equally by their clients. It was clear that the examination procedure needed to be a balance of testing knowledge and assessing practical skill and experience. Since consultants have come to their profession by a variety of routes, not all of them academic, the procedure had also to take into account qualities of character, professional integrity and personality.

Several determined attempts were made to accelerate matters. In 1971 the IMC Council reported in a policy statement that it had decided that 'written examinations should be introduced as soon as a satisfactory procedure has been approved and that the present interview system be maintained as an important part of the intake procedure'. A newly constituted examinations committee under the chairmanship of Anthony Frodsham prepared a complete set of examination papers consisting of two three-hour papers. Four members of the Institute volunteered to sit those examinations and four senior men agreed to mark them. Each of the eight participants then fed back his opinion to the committee in writing. The outcome was satisfactory. As a result, the Council then hoped to be able to introduce examinations for full Membership in 1973. This was not to be. The scheme was found to be unacceptable to rank and file members and was thrown back into the melting pot.

There are three grades of membership in the Institute. In order of rank these are Fellows, Members and Associates. Applicants are eligible to sit the Associate Membership Entrance Examination under the present rules, provided they are over 25 years of age and have served for not less than six months in the independent practice of management consulting at the time of their examination. Members have to be aged at least 30 and normally to have served at least three years under the guidance of a Fellow or Member of the Institute who will verify that service. Fellows have; in the opinion of the Council, to have served the Institute and the Profession with distinction.

The next attempt, after the 1973 debacle, to bring in a compulsory examination procedure was made in 1977. A revised scheme, this time intended for new entrants, was introduced on a test basis in October of that year. The results were correlated against the normal interview procedure two months later. In March 1978, Geoffrey Buss who at the time was Chief Examiner reported to the Council as follows: 'The correlation was considered most satisfactory, the two best candidates on the written papers being also the most satisfactory at interview.'

Entry by examination

Despite acceptance of the more gradual approach, there followed two more years of investigation and testing before a compulsory written examination procedure was introduced. However, since 1 May 1980 all applicants for Associate Membership have had to pass a written examination. The first of these compulsory examinations was held on 24 November 1980 in London and Manchester and on 6 April 1981 in London and Dublin. A total of 38 candidates sat the examination of which 30 were admitted to Associate Membership.

There are three main sectors in the examination syllabus. Section 1 relates to the environment and practice of management consultancy and includes such aspects as: consultant-client relationships: ethical standards; and developing consultant skills. Section 2 relates to business appraisal and implementing change. It includes such aspects as the client's problem and its interpretation; agreeing objectives and action and monitoring progress and performance. Section 3 relates to the application of specialist skills and includes the role of the specialist in management and the management of the specialist function.

One of the main findings from the examination procedure has been that it successfully separates technicians from consultants. The distinction is a fine one but nevertheless considered to be essential. Geoffrey Buss explains,

> You do get people who claim to be consultants who are really purely technicians. They have no understanding of business as a whole. You do not have to be able to operate in all areas, this is not expected, but you should understand the interrelationships between them. Some of the questions in the examination are particularly designed for that purpose. The person is allowed to describe their own specialisation but they are then asked to describe the impact it can have elsewhere in the business. They are also asked to describe how they would go about ensuring there were no disadvantages and that such opportunities as were there were taken. Some applicants do not understand what the question is about. They cannot understand it because it has never occurred to them to look further than their own area.

The problem with introducing an examination procedure which applies only to new members is, of coure, that a considerable time will elapse before the Institute satisfies the requirement that a majority of its members have been admitted by this route. One estimate is of between 10 and 20 years. Recognition by Royal Charter is therefore still a long way off, possibly outside the professional life of many present members.

Protecting the title

An alternative which is being investigated by two of the Institute's committees at the time of writing, is that of establishing some sort of legal right to the term Registered Management Consultant. This is seen as not carrying as high a standing as a Royal Charter but it would mean that only those who are members of the Institute are entitled to call themselves Registered Management Consultants. This measure is viewed as particularly desirable during the present period of high unemployment. Anyone can offer his services as a management consultant and there are strong incentives for executives between jobs or who have simply been made redundant to style themselves as consultants while they are simply looking for a job.

Current thinking within the Institute is that, if it had a lien on the title Registered Management Consultant and promoted it properly along the lines 'If you want a sound job done – use a Registered Management Consultant', this would be a considerable advantage. It would enable the Institute to exercise more control over the standards of work carried out by the majority of consultants.

Looking even further ahead is the thought that, if registration were introduced, eventually the Institute could offer a form of arbitration between a client company and a member consultant similar to that operating in some other professions. The arbitration service could either be carried out by the president of the day or by someone else acceptable to both parties.

Other new moves being discussed in the Institute's plans for the future involve training. The provision of training facilities is seen as a logical requirement stemming from a compulsory examination procedure and control of standards. A first toe has been dipped in the training arena with seminars on such subjects as marketing and behavioural science. Possibilities of publishing text books and papers are also being studied.

However, the same problems are likely to arise in training and the provision of educational facilities as occurred with the various attempts to introduce examination procedures. Consultants' collective experience is extremely wide and few topics are likely to be of equal interest to all members. It is possibly significant that an award scheme presented by Jim Sandford Smith to encourage the writing and circulation of professional papers had to be discontinued because of lack of entrants.

Impact of independents

On the optimistic side, it has to be recognized that the Institute of Management Consultants is a very different organization now from when it was founded. One of the most significant new developments in management consultancy has been the large numbers of sole practitioners and small consultancy groups which have sprung up during the last few years. Many of these are too specialized to be eligible for the description 'management consultant' as defined by the Institute. However an increasing proportion are finding their way not only on to the membership lists but also on to the Institute's policy-making Council and committees.

In the early days, the Council was composed mainly of members from the larger companies. Any representatives of smaller firms which were there, were very special in the sense that, like O. W. Roskill, they were run by people of very high personal standing. In recent years the Council has become much more representative of the smaller firms. Of the 29 Council members listed for 1980–81, for instance, 13 are outside the ranks of the largest companies. It is generally acknowledged that the arrival of more independent practitioners has had a great deal of influence in increasing the speed with which decisions have been taken in the last few years. The independents are more outspoken and tend to react more swiftly and vehemently than their counterparts from larger concerns. They place a more immediate value on their time and wish to see results from work on committees. There is also evidence that the independents are prepared to devote more energies to strengthening the Institute as a whole. As one Council member put it, 'If you are in business on your own, then being a member of the Institute makes a significant contribution to your reputation.'

There are also practical benefits. One smaller consultancy for instance was able to use the Institute's Code of Practice to support his case as an employer at an unfair dismissal hearing. There are additional benefits for independent practitioners in being able to talk over matters of common interest in a wider forum than their own offices provide.

As a member who is employed by one of the larger companies explained, 'If I want to talk to colleagues, all I have to do is to walk down the corridor.'

Professional register

A number of services have been introduced. A Professional Register was launched by the Institute in 1979 stemming from a proposal made by a group of sole practitioners and small firms. The Register acts as a contact bureau to match prospective clients with members who have appropriate consulting experience. Registration is voluntary and like most such developments, growth has been slow, with about 50 per cent of those eligible choosing to participate at the time of writing.

However, much greater scope for expansion is envisaged for the future. In November 1980, as part of a cost-cutting exercise, the British Institute of Management closed down its longstanding Management Consultancy Services Information Bureau which gives the Institute a clear field for expanding its service.

While it has now been generally accepted as benefiting everybody the Register was seen by some of the larger companies initially as tilting the Institute's axis too far in favour of the smaller practitioners. This, at any rate was the argument some of the bigger companies used to cease paying their employees' subscriptions. They said, in effect, that they did not see why they should subsidize an organization which favoured their competitors.

It is clear that differences between larger consultancies and their smaller counterparts must be resolved if the Institute is to take on a full training function. The burden of supplying educative material must fall on the larger concerns which have long-established procedures to train their own staffs. The differences must also be resolved if the Institute is to promote the services of consultants since the resources to do this can only reasonably be expected to come from the larger practitioners. However, as things stand on the corporate front, the larger companies remain clustered under the Management Consultants Association while the smaller companies and sole practitioners are represented only by the Institute.

Amalgamation?

The question of whether the two organizations should amalgamate has been raised at intervals throughout the lifetime of the Institute rather, as one of those involved put it, 'like the tidal waves moving in and out on a sandy shore'.

Advocates reason that amalgamation would eliminate confusion and make it easier to control the professional conduct of companies as well as individuals. It would also cut down overheads, they say (although it is difficult to see how the tiny premises and staffs with which the two organizations operate could be squeezed down any further). More importantly a merger would save the time and energy of the people who at present sit on the councils of both bodies.

Opponents argue that it would be basically incorrect to merge a professional institute concerned with the knowledge, conduct and competence of its individual members with a body which operates as a trade association.

There is also the industrial relations argument that it would not be in the best interests of both parties to cater for employees and employers in a single organization.

Nevertheless, a merger scheme was very nearly brought to fruition in 1973 when proposals drawn up and agreed by the Institute were rejected by the Association. The Institute Council of the day took notice of additional arguments which were that amalgamation would increase membership and release more funds for the promotion of the profession. The Council also pointed out in answer to criticisms from Institute members that under the proposed merger, the Institute would have remained a body of individuals – firms would have had no corporate membership. There would have been a Professional Practices Committee with representatives on the Council to deal with all matters concerning firms as opposed to individuals.

The merger concept has now been revived; and at the time of writing active discussions are again taking place between the two organizations. Two major changes have occurred since the 1973 set of talks which may accelerate matters. One is the departure of PA, by far the biggest single consultancy firm in the country, from the

Association's ranks shortly after the 1973 merger talks broke down. The reason given at the time was that the Association's rules prevented PA from promoting itself through advertisements but it is understood that the company would be sympathetic to a single professional entity. The company has remained a staunch supporter of the Institute and could reasonably be expected to increase its support if it had a more general educational and promotional function.

The other major change has been in the composition of the profession. The very large proportion of sole practitioners which have started operating during the last few years means that, despite the relaxation in its entry requirements, the Association is becoming less representative of the industry as a whole.

The impressive fact that 3,000 individuals feel it sufficiently worthwhile to subscribe to the Institute and to undertake to abide by its Code of Conduct indicates that management consultancy has come a long way to achieving professional status in its own eyes. Considerable strides have also been made, particularly in the last few years, to win Government recognition – notably through the introduction of a compulsory written examination procedure. The kernel which remains to be cracked, however, is that of obtaining professional recognition for clients. As Roger Falk who at the time was the Institute's president pointed out very clearly in a paper delivered to an international conference of management consultants in 1972, 'To become more professional we should not only improve our standards but be seen to be doing so.'

7
What Do They Do?

The type of work management consultants can do for their clients falls into three broad categories. They can operate in a purely advisory role on, for instance, matters of strategic policy; they can inject extra executive manpower on a temporary basis; and they can act as facilitators to help their clients help themselves. Some assignments require all three categories of assistance, others do not.

Without betraying any confidences, the management consultant can bring a body of practical knowledge distilled from a portfolio of similar cases to bear on a situation which a single company might encounter only once in a lifetime. To be accepted as a professional, as defined by the Institute of Management Consultants, a management consultant must also have identifiable expertise in at least one of the fields of business activity recognized by the Institute. These are currently defined as:

Business administration
Company policy and development
Distribution and transport
Economic and environmental planning
Finance
Marketing
Personnel
Production
Information systems and data processing

The consultant will normally form a bridge between academic research in his particular field or fields and its applications in business. Above all, though, he can bring an unbiased fresh approach in providing options against which specific management decisions can be taken.

The professional management consultant ultimately expects a change for the better to result from his activities. However the decision to act has to lie with the client company. Where a lot of users of management consultancy services go wrong is to expect them to operate as substitute managers. A commitment to change is, many experts argue, an essential prerequisite before calling in a consultant. Once the decision in principle has been taken, the consultant can use his persuasive negotiating skills to overcome the resistance to change which lies within every organization.

Changes resulting from consultancy work are not always quantifiable. The modern approach to a management consultancy concentrates as much on human attitudes within the client organization as on tangible benefits immediately arising from changes in layout or manning levels. Many consultants, particularly in sole practices and small groups also aim nevertheless to produce a measurable gain which more than covers their fee if at all possible.

Tangible benefits

One medium sized consultancy which specializes in researching overseas sales territories for instance, likes to bring back some actual orders and a short list of distribution agents alongside its recommendations. Its philosophy is to work alongside a representative from the client company when conducting a study overseas. A report from his own employee not only adds weight to the consultant's recommendations for the client – it also gives him an executive with the skills necessary to carry on where the consultant leaves off.

Sometimes the changes can be unpredictable. Success, particularly in smaller companies, can result from entrepreneurial hunch, flair, or simple bloodymindedness overriding all known logical considerations. By identifying and setting out the logical options in an orderly way, a management consultant may trigger this mechanism and thus 'create a change for the better' even though his recommendations are apparently ignored.

Solutions have to match the requirements of the individual organization's management style. A senior consultant in a large practice speaking about management problems in diversified companies identified two common trends which on occasions he had to counteract. One was a tendency for managers to put too much time and money into the unprofitable parts of their business. The other was to try to get into businesses they knew little about instead of sticking with those which they know.

> One client of mine was in electrical and electronic engineering. This client was a technical enthusiast. He saw that much of his heavy electrical products were becoming obsolete with the trend of newer electronic technology. Of course, trying to make a heavy electrical engineering company into an electronic one is a formidable and expensive task. My contribution was to curtail my client's enthusiasm – to point out that there was still several years' life in the old products and that he should not get bored with them too soon – particularly as some of his competitors with an equal eye for the future were getting out of the obsolescent market – leaving a greater share of it for my client.

Even though tangible, the results of consultancy work may be invisible because they are kept secret. Although extremes of coyness are starting to wear off, most private British companies are still reluctant to publicize the utilization of management consultants' services at strategic policy level. Until recently, the boards of British companies were firmly closed to outsiders of any kind. There still appears to be a suggestion in many directors' minds that by calling in consultants they are somehow making an admission of failure.

There is also understandable worry that an announcement could alarm shareholders by indicating that the company was in financial trouble, alert competitors, or stir up industrial unrest.

However justified or not these concerns might be, secrecy can hamper the consultant by forcing him to work in a cloak-and-dagger fashion. Suspicion and resentment amongst executives in the client company can lead them to feed him with incorrect information.

Relationships with clients

In the illustrative engagements listed by member companies in the Management Consultants Association's handbook strategic policy assignments are sometimes described as 'Advised Chairman'. What does this advice entail? It can range from counsel about his own personal effectiveness to the preparation of a detailed long-term corporate plan. The emphasis of the assignment may be on the consultant's personal relationship with the client in the narrow sense of the person who called him in or the client in the wider sense of the organization itself.

The two are not always in agreement. Consultants are often employed to resolve differences between various components in client organizations. They can be called in to prove or disprove the case put up by one faction or another. They can also be used to endorse unpopular decisions regarding such matters as factory closures or redundancies. Occasionally management consultants are called in as a political weapon in internal rivalries.

Professional management consultants detest becoming embroiled in company politics. Before taking on an assignment they will try to ascertain their immediate patron's motives. If they find they are to be used merely as a whipping boy or a status symbol they will probably refuse the job. On the other hand, they can and do carry out useful work where there are genuine differences of opinion if they can work openly.

By taking a fresh approach and applying his own expertise, a consultant can often identify a third option which had not previously occurred to the resident parties. Even if the solution is not a new one it may prove to be acceptable because it has the blessing of an unbiassed source. Very often the consultant's value is as a catalyst to draw out answers simmering beneath the surface of the client's own company. In his role of facilitator, he can unlock barriers between different company divisions to get the scheme implemented and operating. Sometimes, at the end of an assignment, the client's response is that he has not been told anything that he does not know already. The consultant's reply is then, 'Why have you not done something about it in that case?'

Planning for strategic development

Due to recessionary pressures the bulk of consulting work since the early 1970s has been aimed at cutting costs. But the assignments practitioners in the field enjoy most are those involving an expanding company which wants to accelerate its rate of growth. Through a review of corporate development the consultant can pinpoint ways of, for example, speeding up decisions and improving communications.

The Management Advisory Unit of the Chemical and Allied Products Industry Training Board has carried out a lot of work in this area.

Its conclusions are published in a series of occasional papers under the general heading of Strategic Development of Organizational Change compiled by Jim Green, the manager of the Unit, and Ted Jones, a consultant. One of the aims of the Unit was to identify the training needed to improve the quality of decision-making. It also attempted to discover the 'best' learning approaches to enable the client group to convert the strategy into action and ensure that it achieves change and results.

The unit found considerable variation in the duration of individual strategic projects ranging from 9 to 20 months for small and medium-sized companies while the work content varied from 15 to 60 man days.

One specific project concerned a small company in the Surface Coatings, Adhesives and Mastics Business sector of the industry. In 1978, following a review of their current strategic approach with the six members of the management team of the company, joint work was carried out in building a shared and common view of the 'Present Position'.

This analysis allowed the company to make current strategic decisions regarding the abandonment of certain product groups, critical capital investment in new production facilities and the reorganization of its marketing and sales force.

Through a strategic review workshop run in September 1979, the company has determined its strategic framework over three business areas and has, through the 'Options Analyses' identified the mix of preferred products to give optimum performance for each sector. Agreement was reached over:

(a) Profit objective and growth.
(b) Product range for 1983 – retained products and the introduction of new products with timing;
(c) Actions necessary with regard to new product development embracing production, sales and technical service;
(d) Organizational structure;
(e) Investment.

The strategic plan includes formal declarations relating to trends, assumptions made, options and why they were chosen and strategic action and responsibilities for implementation against an agreed timetable.

Whilst goals have been established, the consultants considered it important that they should also record the short-term benefits and early successes which arose from the 'present position analysis' – the identification of major issues concerning their current performance over finance, marketing, production, distribution and manpower. These were:

(a) Conversion from break-even position to profit earning; systematic reduction of a product because of poor contribution, and the decision to buy-in rather than to manufacture. The space made available by this decision enabled the company to invest in new machinery and improve its existing productivity for meeting a foreseeable market performance in an existing and new product area;

(b) Relative significance of a particular product group/package as a spearhead for strengthening the company's position in a particular market sector;

(c) Reconstruction of the organization and in particular the marketing and selling side, and the restoration of balanced policies between sales and production and supported by greater technical co-ordination and direction regarding potential products and markets.

The secrecy which usually surrounds consultants' activities at corporate strategy level makes the results difficult to evaluate. Consultants operating in this area will, if pressed, point privately to companies which are still in business which they believe would not be trading if it were not for their efforts. They will not name them publicly for obvious reasons.

Alternatively the benefits may be intangible in the sense that they averted a pitfall and to quantify them would be a superfluous exercise. Again, the true benefits or otherwise may not be seen for some time. For instance between five and twenty years may elapse before a strategic development programme for an equipment supplier to, say, the steel or chemical industry can be assessed.

Meanwhile radical changes in the external environment such as unthinkable escalation in energy costs, interest charges and currency exchange rates, to name but a few factors, can distort perfectly valid initial strategies out of all recognition. Modern strategic planning methods incorporate 'sensitivity analyses' to take account of such changes but it will be many years before their effectiveness can be gauged.

The few textbooks which exist on management consultancy stress the necessity for the client to carry out an evaluation. Philip Shay's excellent pamphlet 'How to get the best results from management consultants', although published by the American Association of Consulting Management Engineers in 1974, contains much which is relevant to British users today. It recommends that 'A hard headed evaluation of each consulting engagement should be a regular management practice.' After each engagement, it says, management should review the experience not only from the dollars-and-cents standpoint, but also the intangible results.

Questions the client should ask himself during this process include the following: 'What has happened to internal relations within the company? Have we learned anything about solving this kind of problem which will stand us in good stead next time? Did our personnel get new ideas or approaches and adopt them? Did we uncover problems which we never suspected existed before? Are we off on new paths of activity which show real promise? Have we identified some employee situation of which we were not aware? In short, are we a better, wiser company?'

Specific projects

Easier to assess and therefore to justify and implement than corporate strategy exercises are what one leading British management consultant describes as the 'plumbing' operation where certain specific parts of the client organization are not functioning adequately, for instance, production planning, cost control or marketing. This type of job requires a specialist who will go into the client organization for a short period with a clearly defined specification to introduce the new system and get it working.

Then there are what the same consultant describes as 'fire brigade' types of jobs, where the business is going downhill fast, and as a last desperate throw, consultants are called in. These two categories of work provide the mainstay of British consultancy operations.

A typical example of a successful 'plumbing' job was the reorganization of distribution carried out for the confectionery division of Barker and Dobson in 1977 by Sedgwick Edwards, a small West Sussex-based consultancy practice specializing in physical distribution. The problem was that the company was no longer enjoying the level of trading of the early 1970s. However their production and distribution arrangements had not been altered in response to these changes. The consultants reviewed the existing operation with production originating from three factories destined for customers throughout the UK and in worldwide export markets.

The diagnostic report which was produced by two consultants within five weeks identified a 20 per cent reduction in the existing distribution budget of £1,250,000. It contained four main recommendations:

1 To close the group central warehouse. This had been acquired in a trading boom some five years earlier. Its under-utilized space provided every opportunity for slack practices including low productivity and excessive inventory.

2. To upgrade storage facilities at the factories. The existing practice was to ship finished product to the central warehouse, but with the lower production levels, the consultants spotted the possibility of creating efficient factory depots.

3. To reorganize truck vehicle operations. This would be achieved through the development of a timetabled service between factories and to third party warehouses, linked with full use of articulation. It would be possible to trim the fleet size and operate with younger vehicles which were much more reliable.

4. To redefine the direct delivery requirement.

Were the proposed changes practical? Could the savings be achieved? There were doubts in the company. Questioned closely by the chief executive, the consultants convinced him that their views were realistic. He put them in charge of the implementation team. A six-month action programme was drawn up.

The proposals involved a total of 60 redundancies among warehouse and transport personnel. The unions recognized the need for drastic changes. Their main concern was not over what should be done, but rather that the changes should be carried out fairly.

The consultants achieved their six-month target, with full co-operation of unions and the management. So would it work out? Sedgwick Edwards were retained for a further six-month period to monitor the progress of the new arrangements. A check in mid-1978 showed that in practice savings of £250,000 p.a. had been achieved and the consultants' fees which including expenses totalled less than £25,000 were recovered in a matter of weeks. Customer service had also improved.

This case illustrates the concern which most consultants have with implementation. While the visible result of their activities may be reports and surveys, they see the real key to their profession as persuading the client to act. They bitterly resent the accusation that they draw up fanciful schemes and then walk away from the difficulties of making them work. It is true that consultants take minimum legal responsibility for the consequences of their recommendations but they will argue that this is because the decision and ultimate control of the work rests with the client.

Company rescue

By no means all consultancy exercises have happy endings. An example of a 'fire brigade' assignment which came too late to save the company involves the Bamfords agricultural machinery company which went into liquidation in June 1980. Faced with financial losses exacerbated by high interest charges, strong sterling, industrial disputes and, above all, a declining market for its products, Bamfords called in the P–E Consulting Group which reported with a number of options in November 1979.

Alas, the best that could be offered was a drastic rationalization programme plus an injection of substantial extra equity to make the company more efficient. This would have been at least a two-year project and the consultant could give little assurance of success at the end of it. On examining this option the Bamfords board and its advisers Hambros Bank issued a carefully worded statement saying that 'even with a substantial injection of capital, the long-term profitability of the company could not be assured'. It was not surprising that the bankers 'indicated that they cannot grant the additional facilities which the board and its advisers believe necessary for the company to continue trading'.

Any help P–E could have given in implementing their recommendations was too late for Bamfords. With hindsight it is easy to see that the writing had been on the wall for the company for some time. A study carried out for the EEC on agricultural machinery five years before the collapse identified some of the difficulties.

One of the oldest agricultural engineering companies in the world, Bamfords main product, the baler, was geared to haymaking while agricultural practice had moved increasingly over to silage. Even in haymaking the report concluded that the company 'has been outflanked by Continental developments of drum mowers and rotary star tedders'.

Exercising independence

A professional consultant has to be free to exercise his independence to make recommendations which he believes offer the best solution, even if these are not what the client wants to hear.

A good example is Tesco which brought in McKinsey in 1969 to advise on a move to a new office block. The six months of investigation cost Tesco around £100,000 – and one of the recommendations was that Sir Jack Cohen, the founder and chief executive, should step down. The late Sir Jack who, at 71, was six years past normal retirement age was startled but accepted the advice. What he said at the time was, 'It was quite a shock when the management consultants we put in decided I should go as senior executive.'

Tesco has not employed management consultants since, although Leslie Porter, the current chairman, says, 'They serve a good purpose. For specific purposes they can be very useful. But we use our own, in house.'

Range of services

A great deal of work is still carried out in work measurement, incentive schemes, and operative training where management consultancy has its origins. Here the consultant tends to work on the factory floor as part of a team with the client's executives and staff and with local unions as appropriate, to develop and install new systems and equipment.

But nowadays, management consultants' activities have expanded into sales and marketing, particularly in overseas territories which the prospective exporter has neither the resources nor the expertise to explore for himself. Consultants are very active in computers, robotics and bio-technology. North Sea oil added a whole new dimension as did pressures to conserve energy.

Projects can range in size and complexity from the relocation of a single office to designing a health service for a developing country. Consultants may work alone, in teams under a supervisor, or with associates. A big consultant may also work in partnership with architects and engineers to build and run a really large project such as a power station or an advance factory until the client can take over. The variety of jobs is endless.

The difference between a management consultant and a straight-forward specialist in any given area is that the management consultant will look behind the symptoms to the causes and forward to the consequences of his project on other areas of his client's business. To stop a single project developing into an endless chain the prospective user needs to clearly define the areas he wants examined and the results he expects to achieve. Preferably this should be written down and agreed by the executives responsible.

The British Institute of Management's checklist 'The Effective Use of Management Consulting Services' lists five questions which companies should ask themselves before deciding to seek an outside consultancy.

WHEN CAN CONSULTANTS HELP?
1. Are you facing particular difficulties and would welcome:
– an external opinion and impartial advice?
– assistance in solving them?
2. Have you a specific project but:
– inadequate staff time available?
– insufficient specialist knowledge necessary?
– no permanent need for such resources?
3. Do you feel that 'things are going wrong' but are not clear precisely what the key issues or real causes and possible solution are?
4. Even if you have no immediate problems do you consider that it would be helpful to have a review of methods and systems etc. in order to keep ahead?
5. Before considering the possible use of consultants:
– have you thought through your difficulties as far as you can?
– have you considered whether you can overcome them by using existing resources? (Management services)
– have you considered employing a specialist to act as internal consultant on this and other problem areas?

Care in selection

Once the decision has been taken to go to an outside consultant and the area of operation defined and agreed, the prospective client is then faced with the daunting task of choosing whom to approach. Usually a consultant is called in because the client organization either wishes to make changes or is being pushed by external pressures. The most typical pressures are falling profits, but others could be bad industrial relations, late invoicing, inadequate production facilities, a high wastage rate or an outmoded product. If the pressures are urgent and immediate – as is often the case – the client is vulnerable to the first fast-talking salesman who offers a solution. At this point, before opting for the first name dropped by an acquaintance, he should remember that anyone, no matter how incompetent, can call himself a management consultant.

The Institute of Management Consultants has combined with the British Institute of Management and the Management Consultants Association to provide a more scientific solution. A telephone call to the Registrar at the Institute will produce free of charge a short list of up to six consultants who are qualified and who have indicated interest and availability. The Professional Register which was started by the Institute in 1979 operates on an ingenious system devised by Alex Morley-Smith, the General Secretary. The system automatically sorts consultants by field of specialization and by size according to the enquirer's requirements. It also incorporates a queuing system to share enquiries fairly amongst members.

Unlike the Management Consulting Services Information Bureau which was operated by the British Institute of Management until November 1980, the new joint system is not based on user assessment reports. The only recommendation the Institute will give is an assurance that the consultants are full members and therefore abide by its Code of Practice and have had at least three years in independent practice.

This is partly because of lack of resources to carry out checks and update information but partly, also, because the Institute believes strongly in what consultants call 'warm blooded' contact. It believes that compatibility on a person to person basis is essential between consultant and client if the relationship is to be a productive one. It is anxious to promote contact to establish whether or not compatibility exists at the earliest possible stage.

In response to an enquirer's request for a management consultant, the registrar draws up an anonymous, four-line job specification on an enquiry card. In addition to the description of the job the registrar likes to know the urgency, the location and whether the assignment is at a preliminary, authorized or planned stage. The enquiry card is then sent out to the six consultants which the system identifies as both suitably qualified and next in the queue. Those consultants who indicate that they are interested in the assignment and would like more details are sent a copy of the enquirer's written confirmation while the prospective client is given the names and addresses of the consultants.

The Institute bows out at this stage, leaving it to the enquirer and the consultant to make contact direct. It follows up only to check if an assignment has materialized in order to adjust its records.

The register has a number of limitations. Although growing, only about 300 consultants have registered at the time of writing. A weighting built into the system to give small companies fair representation means that it covers about 1,200 individuals. Therefore, there are about 800 reputable and well qualified consultants within the Institute's membership alone whom it is not possible to contact via the register.

Secondly, the register gives only the barest of introductions. It is up to the prospective client to check out the shortlist relative to his own organization's requirements. Vetting consultants can be a time-consuming and expensive business. Even when a suitable company has been identified, the prospective client should make it his business to meet the individual operating consultant who will be working on his particular assignment.

The young consultant who comes to design and install the computer system may be very different from the consultant who drew up the initial proposal.

Business getting

It is not surprising that companies tend to go back to consultants whom they know and have worked with before even if these may not be technically the best qualified for the job. Throughout consultancy the proportion of repeat business is high – the Management Consultants Association estimates it at about 70 per cent and for some individual practices the proportion is even higher.

Most of the big consultancy firms maintain business development sections whose job it is to contact existing and prospective clients with varying degrees of hard salesmanship techniques, depending on the style of the firm. Techniques range from attendance at social functions to sales letters directly offering the consultant's services. Then there are reports, surveys, articles and books designed for general publication. Consultancy is still a young occupation and its practitioners continuously experiment with marketing their services.

While the Association promotes consultancy on a general front, the Institute's register is the first collective attempt made by consultants to market their services more directly.

The big consultancies look at new business development as an investment in the future. They claim that it would be shortsighted and against their own best interests to talk a prospective client into a service he does not want or need. They maintain they would rather turn down an assignment which was not quite appropriate in the hope that the prospective client might return on another occasion.

A prospective user should not be frightened of responding to an approach by one of the big consultancies. While the service should not be abused, the diagnostic survey which most consultancies provide can give a valuable insight into a business. Diagnosis tends to be allocated to the senior members of a consulting organization. They will be chosen for their broad general knowledge of all management areas and their ability to relate to chief executives of client organizations.

The purpose of the diagnostic survey is to examine the client's assessment of the problem and identify the opportunities for improvement and the resources needed to achieve them. When it is completed, the consultant should have sufficient information to make a proposal which should include an estimate of the duration and cost of the assignment.

Diagnosis

Identification of the real nature of the problem is a highly skilled part of the consultancy process. Different groups within a company, for example, will naturally see the problem in different ways. An example quoted in consultancy circles to illustrate this concerns a service company which had a problem that manifested itself in a large number of initial enquiries by clients, but an exceptionally low take-up figure. Moreover, the take-up figure kept decreasing.

The problem as seen by the sales department was that the service providers, who incidentally were highly technically skilled, did not adjust themselves rapidly to market requirements and were providing the wrong form of service.

On the other hand, the problem as seen by the service givers was that the sales force were dumb and did not understand the technicalities of the service provided and so sold the wrong service. Identifying the real problem in this case was very difficult especially in view of the exceptionally high degree of internal politics leading to lack of co-operation by the staff. The problem, when identified, was a breakdown in communication channels between the sales manager and the service manager who were both competing for a single vacant seat on the board. This breakdown in communication ensured that other groups in the organization suffered and a lot of time was spent in identifying the source of the problem.

The moral of this is to open communication channels with as many groups and departments as are likely to have any bearing on the problem and to listen carefully to what is being said. The consultant must use all his marketing ability to sell the existence of the problem to the people involved, right through the company from middle and lower management to shop-floor level.

If the problem appears at first sight to be in the accounting system then the most important group who should be 'sold' the problem is the accounting staff. Similarly a problem of bad industrial relations 'should be "sold" to shop stewards and production managers'.

'During the "identification of problem" phase the change agent should attempt to determine the power groups within the organization, and try to get the involvement of all the groups likely to be associated with the problem. It is possible, due to the wide experience of the consultant, that he has already identified the real problem ahead of those involved, however, this is probably quite rare and co-operation by the staff of the company can prove invaluable.'

Methods of diagnosis will vary depending on the nature of the assignment and the consultancy concerned. This particular example has been chosen for the thoroughness of its approach. At present diagnostic surveys are normally free, if they can be carried out quickly.

But a number of firms are considering making a charge for this part of their services. Peter Bridgman, Managing Partner of Urwick Orr recalls an instance where his company was asked to submit a proposal for a computer assignment. 'We did not spend all that much time on it, I admit, we did not do a preliminary survey or anything of that sort, but I suppose it all added up to three or four days of consultancy time. This was sent off and one day one of my colleagues phoned up, not having heard anything. The secretary said "Oh, I'm sorry I haven't written to you yet. I've got 26 of these letters to write." That particular client company, a retail organization in the North East, had gone out to no less than 26 consultancies.' Bridgman believes that prospective clients should have meetings with numbers of consultants, select two or three, and be prepared to pay for the diagnosis submitted by those two or three, especially if the client is a professional buyer of consultancy services.

Fees

Management consultancy services are not cheap, but they may not be as formidable as the many myths and legends which surround the business make out.

Fees are usually based on the number of consultant hours or days provided. The rate varies depending on the type of assignment. Consultants who carry out diagnosis and policy development programmes are paid more than those who provide a more technical service. Large organizations with higher overheads and greater resources cost more than a sole practitioner.

As should already be apparent, there is no such thing as a typical assignment. However a rough and ready calculation can be made on an assumption of a fee rate of £300 per day (1981 prices) and assuming a utilization rate of 65 to 70 per cent of total time which would produce an annual chargeable total of 180 days a year. A quotation based on a day or hour rate will usually be accompanied by an estimate either that total fees will not exceed a certain figure or give a maximum-minimum range.

Occasionally, particularly for Government work, a fixed sum will be quoted. This has the advantage for the client that it enables him to budget precisely, but the disadvantage for the consultant that it is inflexible. In a cynical article in *The Director* magazine a few years back, Tony Manley gave using up an agreed budget as one of the reasons why consultants should not be used:

> Any firm with a budgetary system, and this may apply also to government and local authorities, may be sorely tempted around October time to dream up an assignment which will neatly absorb this year's budget for consultancy. When this happens, the bewildered consultant may be observed hastening round the enterprise asking everybody, in a subtle way, of course, whether they have any clear ideas as to what he is supposed to be doing. Any reasonable suggestion will be pounced on by the consultant, and he will do a solid worthwhile job on it.

Fixed budgets could exacerbate this tendency.

Another method of arranging fees is via a retainer, usually on a monthly basis, whereby the client reserves a certain amount of the consultant's time. While he may be paying for time he does not use this has the advantage for the client of ensuring the availability of the consultant's services. Consultants however tend to be restless creatures, trained to work in project mode with a defined start and finish. They themselves will say they tend to lose their 'cutting edge' if more than about one year is spent on one assignment if it is a continuous process. The retainer system can have disadvantages in terms of effectiveness as well as cost and is used less nowadays than previously.

While all consultants are prepared to justify their fees (many express sorrow that they are not asked to do so more often by client organizations) they will resist any suggestion of payment by results. They argue against it on the grounds that it could compromise their professional integrity through focussing attention on short-term gains which might not be in their client's long-term interests. The apocryphal story is told about a group of consultants who, when pressed to produce results before collecting their weekly pay cheque, dashed round a client's factory changing all the light bulbs to a lower wattage!

Most professional consultants have a highly developed sense of business ethics. If they do not believe their clients can more than recover their fees, they will usually not agree to operate. While the overall results may be apparent to everybody concerned it could be extremely difficult to separate out the consultant's contribution from that made by the client organization.

The disadvantage of time-related charges however is that they open the profession to persistent accusations of unduly prolonging assignments to collect more revenue during lean periods. All professional consultants fervently deny such charges and although they persist they have become more muted. In any case they reflect more on the client organization, who should make it its business to set limits than on consultants.

In addition to the fee, there will be a charge for out-of-pocket expenses which may include such items as travel, living expenses and also such services as typing, charting and, possibly, special research. One rule of thumb estimate sets these at 15 to 20 per cent of professional fees although obviously they will vary considerably depending on location, type, and urgency of the assignment.

To obtain a true cost of the service, the prospective user also needs to add his own executives' time and that of whatever office accommodation is required on his premises. The total bill may well lead him to the conclusion that management consultants are very expensive indeed if taken in isolation. If taken against a 20 to 30 per cent reduction in overhead costs or a comparable improvement in volume of output, however, they could appear economical. Add such improvements to the ability which the client organization should have learned to repeat the process on its own and consultancy costs can pale into insignificance. The secret is in defining the job which the consultant is to do, using him properly, and getting him out at the end of it.

8
How Do They Do It?

Techniques and formulae

It is only human to wish for a magic wand, a secret formula, a spell to turn a frog into a prince. Business managers are as human as anybody else in their search for a universal cure for industrial illness. But it is this tendency which has led to the wholesale and sometimes blind adoption of the techniques which are so much a management consultant's stock in trade and also to subsequent disillusionment.

Fashions exist in business purchases just as much as in the consumer area. At one time the computer carried similar status symbol connotations in industry to those of the colour television set in domestic terms. It is a characteristic of fashion that, suddenly for no single reason they can identify, everybody wants the same thing at once in a spontaneous chain reaction. Sometimes the fashion sticks. Sometimes it vanishes. Electronic pocket calculators went through a fashion wave – and stayed. But whatever happened to the skateboard?

Fashions can be sparked by an advance in technology or they can represent a mass reaction to an environmental change, e.g. high energy prices have made thermal underwear into a trendy topic of drawing room conversation. They can be a concept. Remember the 'I'm backing Britain' stickers of the 1960s?

The fashion phenomenon, with its chain reaction of communication, is the fastest known method of introducing change. In business, management consultants whose fundamental reason for existence is that of introducing change are the natural harnessers of such a powerful force. The communication skills which all successful management consultants must possess enable them to 'repackage'

complex abstract formulae into the type of simple, easily compre-
hensible terms which can be adopted as a fashion.

The Bedaux System of work measurement of the 1920s and 1930s
was an early example of consultancy-led management techniques.
Later came Organization and Methods. Later still in the 1960s came
Management by Objectives. At the time of writing, Quality Circles
are showing signs of becoming a cult. Management consultants
themselves became a status symbol for a time.

The problem with fashions is that they die. Moreover not only
does the impetus fade as quickly and as mysteriously as it came but it
leaves a residue of scornful resentment. The antagonism to
anything which is considered 'old hat' is just as unreasonable as the
forces which caused the fashion to start in the first place, but it can
be just as powerful. In order for a former fashion to be
re-introduced, there either has to be a sufficient interval of time for
memories to be blunted by nostalgia, or the once fashionable object
has to be altered or 're-fashioned' in some way.

Communicating ideas

There is very little that is new in the organizing and motivating of
people. What is new is the way in which ideas relating to this area
are conveyed. Lt. Col. Lyndall F. Urwick successfully used military
terminology when communicating to both foremen and chief
executives in the early 1950s when compulsory National Service was
still in force. In the 1970s the emphasis was on employee
participation, industrial democracy and worker directors. In 1982,
after the deepest industrial recession in living memory forced
unemployment to the previously unthinkable total of over three
million, the emphasis has changed yet again.

Len Brooks, managing director of Inbucon who prides himself on
taking a businesslike approach to management consultancy, said,
'Three years ago you talked to a client about participation. You
don't talk about participation today. You talk about "improving
performance through people". Yet it is really the same thing. Now
that is not charlatanism. It is identifying, one, the client's needs
and two, his desire to buy.'

Management consultants consistently stress that their function is
not so much in introducing 'black boxes', i.e. new technologies or
business systems – but in 'making them work', i.e. changing

attitudes and behaviour patterns. Management by objectives, job enrichment, work study, are all methods by which this can be achieved but they are only methods.

Len Brooks went on to illustrate how he would tackle the essence of a consulting problem. Rather than talking to his client about participation, 'You really talk to him about how we can motivate his people to concentrate on reducing operating costs and improving the quality of the product.'

Alternatively and more specifically you say to the client, 'To meet Japanese competition you have got to make a quantum leap. Your manufacturing cycle is three months. "Absolute nonsense," you say to the client, "there is no reason why it should be more than three weeks. If you can get it down to three weeks, that is a gigantic step." '

At this point, says Brooks, 'Everybody throws up their arms in disbelief. But if you can really get hold of the people in charge and demonstrate to them, by taking them to Japan or whatever, that first, this is achievable. Second if you can motivate them that it is what they should be aiming for, you can work wonders.'

Management consultants regard techniques or 'approaches' as having a valuable role in helping businesses help themselves. But any idea of a universal solution has been largely discredited in the current pragmatic business environment. It is well recognized that concepts, no matter how elegant, must be adapted to the particular needs and resources of the moment, just as much as computer systems, or advanced technologies.

The methods which management consultants use to introduce change vary with the individual practitioners. The participative approach, where the consultant influences rather than directs, most aptly describes the modern style of consultancy. Some consultants, however, may perform better in an authoritarian role, particularly if quick changes are needed among people who are dependent rather than independent. In either event, the consultant needs to be trusted. He should not only be an expert but be introduced and recognized as one.

Once he has generated trust and won the attention of his target audience, the consultant may use one of a number of behavioural science-based methods or a combination of several to achieve his objectives. One common method is to analyse and set down both the known reasons for the proposed change and the known objections. The consultant will then concentrate on and try to resolve the resistances which would otherwise counterbalance the move towards change.

Theories about change

Management Consulting, the International Labour Office's guide to the profession, describes this process in detail in a chapter on 'Consulting and Change'. It says:

> In presenting a given proposal in preference to alternative schemes, it is often necessary to mention some negative aspects of the proposed scheme in addition to the more beneficial ones.
>
> Similarly the positive and negative aspects of existing or alternative schemes should also be presented. This technique of providing all aspects of the case under review is referred to as inoculation effect which weakens any counterproposals likely to arise at a later date. Experience has shown that an effective manner of presenting information where proposal B is intended to displace proposal A is to employ the following sequence:
> 1. Present a complete listing of the positive, beneficial aspects of proposal B;
> 2. Mention the obvious and real drawbacks associated with proposal B;
> 3. Describe a comprehensive listing of the deficiencies of proposal A;
> 4. Indicate the most pertinent positive features of proposal A.
>
> Following this presentation of the positive and negative features of the alternative proposals, the consultant should then draw conclusions as to why the favoured proposal (B) should be employed by listing the benefits to be accrued (i.e. service provided); the effectiveness of the new proposal (i.e. technical and economic superiority); and, if applicable, instances where such proposal has been successfully employed.

According to the textbook approach described in *Management Consulting* the 'change event is said to occur with the advent of an influencing agent of repute and prestige (hence the need for the consultant to be both good at his job and acknowledged to be good) operating in partnership with management and workers in the client organization'.

> The sub-processes of changing involve two elements:
> – Identification – where the people concerned recognise the authority of the change agent, adopt his external or generalised motive, test out the proposed changes and, hopefully, accept the general principles of

change; and – Internalisation, where individuals translate the general principles advocated by the change agent into specific personal goals by means of adaption, experimentation or improvisation. The process of internalisation of new goals is often quite difficult, usually requiring a good deal of creativity on the part of the change agent in assisting the change to convert the external (general) to internal (specific and personal) motives for accepting the change proposed.

These processes require commitment, involvement or participation by the person doing the changing. The change must be tested by the individual as he moves from the general (identification) to the specific (internalisation).

Therefore, as early as possible the people concerned in the change process require to be involved, so that these two vital elements can be comprehensively covered. However, a strong note of warning is offered concerning how participation might be achieved. Apart from attending brain-storming sessions employed for specific purposes such as to provide a data bank for ideas for the solution of creative problems, individuals should not be encouraged to seek their own methods of performing tasks if the general idea is to develop a best method as recommended by the consultant. Results of studies show that where individuals are permitted to adopt their own approaches and the best-method or approved solution is later imposed, the individuals will exhibit some conformity to the new proposal, but will still diverge significantly from the approved method in following their own methods.

However, where persons in groups are provided with a best-method or approved approach in the first instance, it is found that subsequently individuals will vary only insignificantly from the set procedures.

The personal touch

While they give a fascinating glimpse into the thought processes, the textbook theories about change do not always work out in real life. The consultant's starting point is his client in the personal sense. Will he accept what Dr Charles Margerison, Professor of Management Development at Cranfield School of Management (Institute of Personnel Management 1978) describes in *Influencing Organizational Change* as the 'situation analysis approach' or is a 'technique push approach' the only one which he will accept? In the former the consultant adviser does not introduce any special new technique. Instead he puts his main emphasis on getting the client to extend his thinking on how to solve the problems related to the task in hand. Alternatively, the consultant can himself opt or 'push' for a particular method or technique and apply it to his client's problem.

The technique approach can be the most appropriate according to Margerison if:

1. The problem has been clearly diagnosed.
2. The client has no interest in spending time working on the problem personally.
3. He is prepared to pay someone else to provide him with a solution without himself understanding how the solution is arrived at.
4. The adviser has special expertise which enables him to do the job more effectively and quickly by himself.
5. The adviser believes that the solution he arrives at will be accepted and implemented by the client, even though the client was not involved in the development of the solution.

Margerison points out that although the choice has to be made between the two approaches the consultant will continually be faced with the dilemma of whether he has made the right one.

For example the client may say, 'Look, I can't waste a lot of time on this. What I want you to do is to go away and produce a training policy for me. You've done this many times before for other companies. I am sure you can let us have a document without wasting a lot of our time discussing the matter.' At this point the adviser has to decide whether he will accept the brief and take it away or try to work with the client in a joint problem-solving way.

In her work as social scientist with the Esso Company, Lisl Klein describes how the dilemma of when to continue task analysis and when to push techniques faced her on a number of occasions. A study of the distribution operation at Purfleet was undertaken. A meeting with the terminal manager and his staff was held to report back the findings. Klein (in *A Social Scientist in Industry*, Gower Press 1976) then outlines what happened and her reactions: 'At the end of the meeting the manager said that they had all much appreciated the report and discussion. He then drew back a little and added that this was all very well, but he could not be expected to make changes without quantitative information. How real, for instance, was the planners' complaint that they had too much to do? What actually was the work content and workload? Would it be possible to mount a study to back up insight with figures? We needed a detailed analysis of the work of the Planning Office, but with the right kind of categories of the kind you've raised. Above all not an O and M study, that would be comptroller and accounting-orientated.

'For a second or two, I debated whether to agree to this. At one level [it] seemed an avoidance of responsibility and a manoeuvre to put the ball back into my court and postpone coming to grips with the problems. At another level it was reasonable. We did have very little factual information and everyone at the meeting, including the planners, felt [it] would be valuable to know exactly what went on in the Planning Office.

Was it right for Klein to collude or agree with the manager's request[?] Was it an issue that needed to be confronted?

In her own review of the situation, Klein later reflects that it was the appropriate thing to do although acknowledging that it could be seen as collusion with a client who was playing for time and avoiding the issue.

'If you confront the client, are you trying to pressurize the client to do what you want against his will or just help avoid the errors he will commit and regret out of ignorance . . . The dividing line is a narrow one,' Margerison concludes. 'You have to make quick decisions and live by them. Do you confront the client and risk a power struggle or collude and risk error and waste?'

Although the example relates specifically to personnel matters, it gives a vivid illustration of the dilemma which also faces management consultants when dealing with their clients. It is interesting in that it contains the trained observations and subsequent analysis of a social scientist by an industrial sociologist.

Dr Margerison, in addition to having taught widely in Europe and North America on the applied behavioural science aspects of business, has worked with a number of large companies as an adviser on management and organization development problems. He recognizes very well the worries that most client companies may have about the open-ended implications of situation analysis. 'Where will the process lead to? At least when one enters into a job enrichment, management by objectives, discounted cash flow or other programme, there are reasonable limits. Also, one usually feels one knows what is being bought – even if this turns out not to be exactly what was expected,' is how he expresses the client reaction.

The use of persuasion

The art of persuading people to participate in the process of change is probably the most mysterious aspect of the consultants' work as far as outsiders are concerned. It is their activities in this area which have surrounded management consultants with the aura of witch doctors – a reputation which they have been trying to shed throughout most of the last two decades. Yet the principles of occupational or industrial psychology, behavioural science or simple human relations have been the subject of scientific investigation ever since the turn of the century. The Hawthorn experiments which showed that workers respond to interest and attention with improved productivity were carried out in the late 1920s. The NTL (National Training Laboratories) Institute for Applied Behavioral Science has been in operation in the United States since 1947 and its concept of the T Group (T for training) where individuals work in small groups in order to understand how groups operate and how individuals interact with groups, have been widely imitated.

While some have particular skills in this area, all management consultants use elements of behavioural science in achieving change. A senior consultant practising with one of the big firms explains why this is necessary. 'Generally speaking, if you introduce change using a route which does not involve people and has not enabled you to get a group of people who are in that changed position, who understand about it, then there is a danger of the change dissipating. As soon as things get difficult people will disown the new method as coming from outside, Head Office, or whatever, and nothing to do with them.'

Behavioural sciences

Although they may be described differently, behavioural science-based methods are applied by consultants at all levels in client organizations from shop floor to boardroom. A traditional application is in industrial relations. Paul Johns, a senior consultant at Urwick Orr and Partners, gave a detailed description of the consultant's role in helping management and unions introduce change at an Institute of Personnel Management Conference a few years ago (*Productivity Improvement – Tell, Consult or Bargain?*, 1980).

Johns' experience is that conflict can be minimized and change accepted more readily if the negotiation of terms is preceded by a joint problem-solving exercise. The aim is to establish and define the maximum common ground between all concerned before negotiation takes place. Problem-solving discussions are organized through working parties or project groups which, in addition to representatives of the interested parties, may include individual experts, and consist of between four and eight people. These are linked by a steering committee.

Once management and each union group has taken stock of the company's problems, and their own, discussions proceed in planned stages. The consultant's role is that of providing guidance and training. He will have had the experience of having 'been down this road before' knowing the likely hazards and ways round them. He can act as an independent arbitrator or referee since he is detached. He is not an heir to the industrial relations history of the company and has nothing to gain or lose in terms of power.

The consultant can apply his skill to explain the concepts under discussion in ways that are intelligible and relevant to managers and union representatives. He will also probably have specific skills in areas such as teamwork training, analysing facts and preparing reports. Finally, he can apply 'push' as a project leader or co-ordinator.

To illustrate the effects of a joint problem-solving approach Johns gave the following case history:

A textile company employing 650 people was suffering from low productivity due mainly to outdated manning levels on key machines and a counter-productive bonus scheme – both stoutly defended by the union. Also a complex assortment of job rates and allowances inhibited flexible use of manpower and caused a great deal of fragmented bargaining department by department, with management tending to react to industrial relations events as they cropped up. By following a strategy of 'joint problem-solving before negotiation',

1. Management and union reached a common understanding that talks about methods and manning would be kept separate from talks about pay; and that an agreement on pay structure should precede negotiations over pay rates.

2. The board prepared a statement of the company's intentions in industrial relations. These included 'the continued search for higher productivity; high, stable earnings and fair differentials; the practice of consultation before negotiations' which the managing director discussed with all employees in groups.

3. Management and union then held a series of discussions which

resulted in an agreement on 'high earnings and high productivity' including a programme of work study to establish methods and manning and a plan for a simplified pay structure; this agreement was also discussed with groups of employees.

4. Agreement was subsequently reached on new manning levels, which were achieved over 18 months by cancelling vacancies and voluntary redundancy; and on new rates of pay.

5. This resulted in lower costs and higher earnings, and the industrial relations climate was greatly improved by the increased mutual understanding and the habit which developed of:

– clearly separating talk about methods from talk about pay
– keeping all employees informed of developments.

All the traditional management consultancies have had considerable experience in industrial relations. Urwick Orr is certainly not unique in helping companies to improve productivity, pay structures or employee relations – or some combination of all three. Usually the key to success has been in getting management and union representatives (often from different unions) to work together in introducing specific changes such as new manning arrangements or a new pay structure. Management consultants experienced in industrial relations understand very well the sort of conflicts which can develop between management and unions, e.g. 'Your productivity improvement is our redundancy' and between different union groups, e.g. 'When your bonus increases our differential is eroded', and can identify them quickly.

They also have access to knowledge which may be locked in a company (e.g. fitters can know a great deal about how machine down-time can be reduced; systems experts can devise more effective ways of monitoring it) but which may not be conveyed to the decision takers along conventional communication channels.

The boardroom viewpoint

Management consultants, however, do not always agree as to the best answer to any question. Nor do their solutions always work. Sir David Nicolson, who worked his way through the P–E Group and chaired it for five years from 1963, maintains that management consultants cannot really understand top level policy and organizational changes unless they have had practical experience of running a company. While he still considers that he practises elements of his old craft, Sir David moved out of consulting to spend more than ten years chairing the boards of different companies including British Airways, BTR and Rothmans International. He has therefore seen consulting work from both sides of the boardroom table.

Management consultants are frequently engaged to produce a new structure plan when companies are merged. Rothmans International had called in a leading American consulting organization to advise on the amalgamation of four separate international tobacco groups in 1972, three years before Sir David arrived to take over the chair. The management consultants' approach was to set up a new headquarters separate from any of the component companies with its own managing director and central functional staff.

The structure was theoretically efficient but in practice it produced new problems of isolation and communication. Sir David applied a different tactic. He analysed the fundamental problem as a human one. Apart from their national characteristics the various companies had radically different management styles and structures. For example, the German company had always been independent with different systems and good cash reserves. The Belgian company had its own outside shareholders. 'It was quite clear that the first problem was to get these chaps to trust each other and to work together before you talked about anything to do with scientific management,' Sir David says.

What he did was to set up central committees dealing with production, marketing, finance, research and development and purchasing. The committees consisted of executives from the various companies and each had a chairman of a different nationality. The functional groups worked on specific topics and gradually the atmosphere in the company improved sufficiently for Rothmans International to set up central financial control mechanisms and other unified departments. 'Often, you know, you have to bend the theory,' Sir David comments. 'If you are actually running a big company, you may have to do things which are not according to the textbook, but which you know are going to be a step towards where you want to get to ultimately.'

Political barriers

Consultants can analyse a problem correctly and design the right solution but when it comes to implementation, schemes can be twisted out of all recognition or shelved altogether by weak management or bad industrial relations. An assignment carried out while Sir David was chairman of P–E provides a typical example of how consultancy work can be wasted.

The assignment involved a survey into the loading and capacity of the Glasgow Corporation's transport department services. The survey, which took six months to complete and cost the department £5,460 (at 1965 prices), discovered that wide discrepancies existed between the public demand and the capacity provided on some routes. The highest load factor was 94 per cent of the seating accommodation on some services while the lowest was 34 per cent. The survey report recommended that services should be tailored more closely to demand. This would have meant reducing the frequencies of many services but by doing so it was estimated that 'a conservative saving' of £780,000 a year could be achieved. The reduction in costs could be used, the report suggested, to finance a bonus scheme of the order of £400,000 a year for the department's 6,000 drivers and conductors leaving a net saving to the department of £380,000.

Despite the gains, the plan was not implemented. A note in the *Glasgow Herald* on 7 August 1965 records, 'A corporation transport services sub-committee decided yesterday that the recommendations would be unacceptable to the travelling public and to the trade unions, and agreed simply to note the report.

'Councillor William M. Lee, transport convener, said the cuts in the services which the report proposed were much too drastic. "We will not be taking the report any further," he said. "If we implemented the proposals it would mean nothing but trouble for the committee, both from the public and trade unions." '

The above is an illustration of the type of assignment which provides the bread and butter of British consultancy work. If the consultancy's diagnosis of the problem and its proposals for a solution are accepted, an operating or resident consultant or a team of consultants will normally move in to work with the client organization in implementing the proposals under the guidance of a supervisor.

Depending on the nature of the assignment the consultant can guide and advise the client's staff. Particularly if new methodology is involved, he may draw up a manual or instruction sheet. He can carry out direct training exercises and monitor progress. He can supervise the commissioning and installation of new equipment or he can take over and run the project until the client organization can provide his own team.

In every case however his aim will be to phase himself out of the organization in such a way that the client company can take over. Professional consultants maintain that they do not perpetuate their assignments by making the client dependent on them. Lyndall Urwick, one of the first of the professional practitioners, maintained that 'The only work that is really worth doing as a consultant is that which educates – which teaches clients and their staff to manage better for themselves.'

9
Profiles

Missionaries and mercenaries

One of the first questions businessmen asked when management consultants appeared on the industrial horizon was, 'Who are these people, and are they any good?' Enough evidence has been accumulated over the years to show that management consultants can be very good for businesses. But conjecture about the type of individual who is attracted to management consultancy and who makes a success of it remains.

The professional consultant's objectivity, while essential to his job, forms a cloak which obscures a clear understanding of his motives. He is neither going to suffer nor to gain from the changes which he facilitates within organizations. Equally, he cannot afford to give complete personal loyalty to any individual within it. As a result, the scientific detachment which enables him to weigh up the consequences of the changes can be mistaken for coldbloodedness and even disinterest.

Another and more formidable obstacle to understanding is a mirror-like quality by which trained consultants reflect the observer's own image back to him. This skill is valuable since the initiation of the change comes from within the client organization and often what is mainly needed for a clearer understanding is a sounding-board. But if developed to the point where it becomes automatic, this reflective characteristic can make the consultant seem rather nebulous as a private individual.

The pioneers of the profession can be grouped into two loose categories: the missionaries and the mercenaries. Both character traits continue to be present in succeeding generations and can make a disconcerting combination. Often consultants themselves are unclear as to which is the predominant motivating factor. The glamorous image and relatively high salaries offered by consultancy firms in the buoyant 1960s attracted large numbers of able and very ambitious young people into the profession. They came in often with the objective of staying for two or three years and then moving on. A surprising number stayed in consultancy, if not with their original employers then by setting up in business on their own. Even within the big firms and in the uninspiring trading conditions of the early 1980s, staff turnover of consultants is only around the 10 to 11 per cent mark. There seems to be a vocation in consultancy which gets under the practitioner's skin and stays there.

Pay and prospects

There is little to attract the mercenary in consultancy within the big firms at present. Prospects for promotion have contracted sharply in the slimming-down processes of the last decade. Although higher than those paid for comparable positions in manufacturing industry, salaries are not exceptional. At 1982 rates, a consultant with one of the large firms aged between 27 and 40 could expect to be paid between £12,000 and £21,000 per annum. Although travel and overheads are covered while he is on assignment, he would expect to receive few other fringe benefits.

Pension arrangements are described as not particularly generous since, whatever the reality, new entrants do not expect to stay for long, and there would be no share of profits. There is little job security. The 1970s proved that consultants, if anything, are even more prone to redundancy than their counterparts in manufacturing industry.

Financial prospects for consultants operating as sole practitioners or in small groups appear to be worse than in the larger firms. Consultants' own research shows that sole practitioners on average earn slightly less than other consultants but work longer hours. Opportunities for career advancement are limited, if not negligible in most cases. Although attitudes to independence have become more flexible, professional ethics still inhibit financial links with non-fee-earning activities. The main source of earned income which is open to a consultant in strictly ethical terms, other than his fees, is from royalties from published material.

Several consultants have written management bestsellers, but increasingly they are meeting with stiff competition from the business schools. Professors dealing in specialist areas but rubbing shoulders every day with able young people are more likely to come up with imaginative ideas than hard pressed fee-earning consultants. They are also often able to communicate their ideas better and are more likely to be able to devote the necessary time to thinking and writing.

Lecturing and writing about management topics has been the traditional method of burnishing a reputation; and consultants have not yet discovered a better alternative method of reaching a wide audience. On the surface, it seems strange that management consultants have not turned to the immediacy of the newer media of television and radio as vehicles to convey their ideas. There is, after all, a strong precedent in the avid use which Frank Gilbreth made of the cinema newsreels of the early 1920s. But modern consultants, both by inclination and by training, are cautious about expressing opinions and hate being forced into making snap judgements. As a result, they are not equipped to sit on either side of the vigorous type of debate which attracts a broadcasting audience.

The basic mercenary and missionary characteristics of the consultant converge over the question of reputation. A good reputation is necessary, not only for pragmatic reasons of sound business practice but also as a requirement for the consultant's own self-esteem. The current social climate which rejects the concept of heroes at all levels, but particularly in business, works very strongly to the consultant's disadvantage. Economically, the continuous accent on producing tangible benefits has exacerbated a tendency towards chronic insecurity. If turned inwards, the management consultant's training in objective analysis and questioning processes can have devastating psychological effects.

Loss of self-confidence in turn tends to create a downward spiral in that it becomes increasingly difficult to win the full support of client organizations. Without full commitment from the client, the consultant's efforts in creating change are less likely to be fully implemented.

Consultants feel themselves to be generally misunderstood. Their own research gives a clear agreement in feelings that the general public is not well aware of their role. About 60 per cent also feel that the profession could do more towards the economic well-being of the country as a whole.

The role of the specialist

Where missionary and mercenary interests conflict is over the question of running a consultancy practice as a business. Financially, the bread and butter of modern British management consulting is provided by the installation and improvement of business systems. The systems may be new to the organizations concerned, but they will be familiar to the consultants whether they deal with computers, accounting procedures, production control methods or some other specialist area. The consultants operate as teams and not as individuals. They adapt and apply existing knowledge but seldom innovate.

Plum jobs for consultancies in this field are the large dimension programmes such as rapid transit systems for congested cities or a health service for developing countries which require considerable technical expertise and many hours of work. Typically, the teams which undertake such projects consist of a multi-disciplined group of consultants working alongside the client's own specialists.

Often much of the design and mathematical analysis work is carried out in the consultant's own office and not on his client's premises.

Management consultants claim that the service they provide differs from those of rival specialists such as software houses, traffic engineers or regional planners in that they can offer a total business solution. Their training, they maintain, gives them an awareness of how different components of a business interlock, how change in one section can have an impact on another. However, as managers have become smarter, and consulting assignments more specific, the differences between the specialists and management consultants have become less and less perceptible.

The role of the generalist

But, supported by the systems activities, rather like jam on the bread, is a different style of management consulting. This is mainly concerned with the persuasion and influencing of people and attitudes but also with original thinking. Because the way such consultants achieve change is by leverage and chain reaction, their contribution is difficult to measure and impossible to quantify in erms of running a consultancy business.

A lot of the most effective changes created by 'pure' management consultants produce only long-term benefits: persuading a tired proprietor to loosen the reins of a dying business; finding and firing the imagination of the right finance director to take on a seemingly impossible tangle of companies; etc. These can give flimsy financial return for months of patient effort which could be technically duplicated by an advertisement and a few hours of interviewing time. The consultant's personal reward is the survival of the business, but the only justification for his employer is the hope that the new management becomes a loyal future customer. A consultant's efforts in resolving a long-standing quarrel between a matron and hospital planners have halved the delay which a construction project would have otherwise encountered. Again, how can this be measured? Yet it is contributions such as these which distinguish the work of a management consultant from the specialist.

'Pure' management consulting is an art rather than science. This is a point on which Sir Roger Falk, a former president of the Institute of Management Consultants and author of *The Business of Management* (first published in 1961 and now in its eleventh edition), feels particularly strongly. The consultants' artistry, in Falk's view, lies in being able to communicate with real conviction. 'This is the point where a cold fact and logic must yield to sincerity and belief,' he maintains. 'I don't believe that a consultant worth his salt can get away with a solution unless he himself believes it is the right one.'

Consultants who are sensitive to human interaction have a role different from that of management in facilitating changes within organizations, he explains. 'All too often, management needs the succour of the outsider who has measured the consequences in a scientific and detached kind of way, and can then help the enlightened chief to put across the logic of his decision to his management. And believe you me, this is an art – this ability to make the client understand that change can often be the sole salvation of an ailing enterprise.'

Even before the grim blow of the 1973 oil crisis, Falk believed there was a real danger of both management and management consulting 'becoming cocooned in their own professionalism and that a kind of spurious technology might well develop and obscure a process which of its very nature is concerned with human skills'. His fears, along with those of many of his counterparts, have been increased considerably by the events of the last decade.

Falk is himself a pluralist of distinction. He has been a member of the Monopolies and Mergers Commission and is chairman of the Sadler's Wells Foundation as well as carrying on sundry other activities in a very active retirement.

Falk entered consultancy in the early 1950s by an unusual route. He was recruited to The P–E Consulting Group by Sir Maurice Lubbock, the founder chairman, to set up a marketing division. Previously Falk, who was then in his forties, had been Director General of the British Export Trade Research Organisation, a publicly funded export promotion organization – after a career which had spanned the manager's office of Rhodesia Railways, the manager of the Bombay and Calcutta offices of D. J. Keymer & Co., and chairmanship of the same company.

'I purposely closed the BETRO when the Korean war started', he recalls, 'because there was no hope of export promotion at the time. People just weren't interested in exports. They had gone back to making uniforms and weapons and raw materials were in short supply.'

As managing director and chairman of the new marketing subsidiary, Falk at first found life in a management consulting firm very strange. This was P–E's first big diversification away from production engineering; and despite direct support from the chairman, Falk with his extrovert attitude to consultancy was regarded with considerable suspicion by his new colleagues. 'The old guard looked on me as some sort of vermin which had inadvertently strayed into a hallowed precinct,' he remembers. 'I was introduced to my colleagues as "This is Roger Falk, be very careful of him, he might try to sell you something." There was this awful fear of somehow vulgarising things – which frankly, I think still lingers.'

When he became chairman of P–E in 1972, Falk had the unenviable task of cutting the number of consultants employed there by about one-third in what he refers to as 'a bit of a surgical job'. But while, with hindsight, he admits to making a gross misjudgement as Chairman in believing that the growth area in consultancy activities in the early and mid 1970s would be corporate strategy, he continues to back the role of the broadly based generalist over that of the specialist for the long-term future of the profession.

He believes that specialist functions which at present provide the financial basis for the consultancy practices ought, in the end, to be taken on board by in-house management, just as work measurement has been largely absorbed. Emphasis on specializations is inevitable during an economic recession, but once the economy gets going again, companies will need to take long looks at themselves. 'That is not going to be done with a board meeting once a month and a bigger contribution from non-executive directors. It has got to be done in a highly concentrated way by first-rate people who have an amalgam of skills and knowledge and experience,' Falk maintains. 'The management consultant cannot afford to keep his horizons narrow. To be a really good consultant he needs to be a rounded individual.'

However well rounded they might be, there are few extroverts visible among the rank-and-file consultants employed by the traditional big firms in the 1980s. Instead, there is a preference for anonymity and a strong disinclination to speak to strangers about clients' affairs. The clampdown on recruitment has brought chief executives back into harness as the leaders of major assignments. Further down the ladder, the main concentration among the older men is on improving and updating their personal specialist skills. The younger consultants who have been recruited mainly for their technical competence and to meet specific client requirements are having to learn about how business operates.

The consultants employed by the big firms conform to a similar pattern. They have been recruited from the same pool of graduates and professionally qualified men (there are very few women) in their early thirties who have had some years of junior management experience behind them. They are chosen for the same traits of personality – liking people and being liked by them is important, as are diplomacy and listening skills. Recruiters of consultants also look for people who are good communicators, articulate, and able to present not only their own ideas but those of their client's management in a coherent and persuasive manner. The ideal recruit should be sufficiently self-assured to inspire confidence but intellectually modest so as to get the best out of the people he is working with.

Once recruited, the consultants are put through similar training.

Usually this consists of about four weeks' formal instruction, followed by several more helping a resident consultant on an assignment, then a further period in the classroom before being turned loose on clients. The typical consultant is methodical and hardworking and is also careful to subdue any inclination he might have towards flamboyance.

The MBO man

An example of an outstanding consultant who is very conscious of the necessity of not becoming bogged down in day-to-day problems is John Humble. Humble has been described as the British father of Management by Objectives – an 'approach' to management development which swept like wildfire through companies on both sides of the Atlantic in the mid-1960s. A British Institute of Management survey in 1969 showed that the number of companies claiming to have applied MBO had risen from about 2 per cent to 20 per cent over a 12 month period although only a small fraction used consultants.

In fact, according to Humble, MBO originated in his friend Peter Drucker's *Practice of Management* published in the early 1950s. In a typical, throwaway paragraph, Drucker wrote, 'The real difficulty lies not in determining what objectives we need, but in deciding how to get them. There is only one fruiful way to make this decision: by determining what shall be measured in each area and what the yardstick of measurement shall be.'

At that time, the concept of breaking down management activities and applying measurements to them was a new one, but Drucker left it to others to develop into a feasible method of management development. Most of the experimentation in management techniques in the 1950s was being carried out in the United States. Humble, while he was operating as a consultant with Urwick Orr, came into contact with the thinking in the US in 1960 when he went there for three months on a Ford Foundation Grant. Management training had always been an Urwick speciality and Humble had already drawn up a number of management schemes which concentrated not on the details of a manager's job, but on the results he undertook to obtain.

Humble explains that he 'got very entranced' in the United States by the 'integration of the various bits of the management process. It seemed to me that the future of consultancy had to lie, at any rate in the foreseeable future, in being able to see the relationship between the parts, not just the parts. Now, MBO was really the vehicle for expressing that feeling.' Humble's first pamphlet on the subject, *Improving Management Performance*, was published by the British Institute of Management in 1965, the same year that George S. Odiorne's *Management by Objectives* appeared in New York.

The concept won more or less instant recognition. On this side of the Atlantic Humble's pamphlet won him an Institute Award and sold some 45,000 copies in its various editions. Banks and government departments extolled its virtues. For Humble it meant that he was boosted into star rating class in management circles, appearing regularly on lecture platforms and in films.

'That became for me and others in the organisation [Urwick Orr] a kind of Walter Mitty time,' Humble recalls. Everything was converging: 'our clients were unconsciously feeling in the same direction, we were leaders in the field and innovated in it, and the organisation became excited about it'.

But, by 1968, the emphasis had shifted from the manager's needs to those of his employer: 'I kicked myself for neglecting the interface between objectives as instruments of management development, and the overall objectives of the company. Combine the two and the manager's desire for self-improvement will mesh with the shareholder's call for profits,' Humble said some years later.

Although appointed to the board of Urwick Orr, Humble says he steadfastly refused to carry out a line management function because 'that was never my thing – I was always a professional'. Even so he found an increasing proportion of his time was being eaten up by internal affairs. 'You can't escape dealing with appraisals and plans and budgets if you are a director of a relatively small business in difficult times.'

This became increasingly irksome because it took him away from interesting assignments which he had negotiated. His feelings that delegating these was 'like giving away ice cream to me' were echoed by many senior consultants at that time. In 1976, at the age of 51, Humble decided to take a chance and 'do his own thing'. He describes his twenty-one years with Urwick Orr as very happy ones, but 'there was more fun around the corner'.

Now operating as a sole practitioner, Humble divides his time into various portions, only one of which concerns his consulting base of about five regular clients. He is very conscious of the dangers, which all sole practitioners face, of capitalizing on past strengths. To avoid these he gives himself a new research project each year 'usually something I think I can't do – just to be sure that the brain is moving'.

Topics he has covered in this way include a review of corporate social responsibilities which helped to win him the Management Centre, Europe's Social Responsibility Award in 1978, and a paper on the general manager in strategic tax management written jointly with John Chown, a tax specialist. During the last two years he has been working out some ideas on profit improvement. He also teaches because 'teaching is really good discipline' and runs seminars 'in order to get ideas out and learn' as well as writing articles and making films.

A personal structure plan is created for each year, with international events such as the MBO Society's annual congress as landmarks. 'However,' Humble comments wryly, 'any nice balance can be easily thrown out of kilter by unforeseen requests for help on projects which are intellectually or professionally exciting enough to be tempting.'

Emotionally he does not find it in the least difficult working on his own. 'I feel no need to rush about and seek the opinions of ten other people.' MBO was unusual in the extent to which it caught the public imagination and Humble says he was lucky in that the reputation which Urwick Orr helped him to build was an asset. Financially, he has no particular worries. He likes a simple life, employs no staff, and works from home using inexpensive equipment. He has enough money for his needs, he says. If he wanted to be wealthy, he wouldn't do research or teach. 'If my only goal was to maximise the number of fee earning days, then, in my case, I suppose I could dedicate myself to doing MBO as it was done ten years ago. There is still an enormous market for it in the developing world. Well, you would become totally sterile, you would get money in the bank, but what is the point of that.'

Accountancy groups

Having snatched the dominant share of management consulting work from the general practices in the 1970s, the accountancy groups are well placed to carry the ball on for at least the rest of the decade. They have, for instance, a natural introduction to the financial services industry sector where organizations such as banks, insurance houses and investment companies are expected to lead developments in information technology in offices – regarded as a prime expansion area for consulting work. There growth and expertise in data processing should ensure growth in other technologically advanced European Economic Community countries.

While any rosiness in the medium term future as far as the organization of management consultants is concerned would appear to lie with specialist groups and accountancy-based practices, the heart of the profession lies with the practitioner as an individual. Here too there are changes on the way.

It is reasonable to speculate that management consultants would be in the vanguard of the changes in status which have affected all management. Two decades ago both managers and consultants regarded their employers as 'bosses'; they worked 'for' rather than 'with' them and 'took orders' rather than 'reported to'. The tendency in both categories is for almost a return to the old craft guilds in that loyalties and values lie more with the profession than the employer. The idea that a consultant, or for that matter a manager, may 'sack' his employer may not be as bizarre as it might sound.

A change in status was, albeit symbolically, recognized by the Institute of Management Consultants in 1976 when it agreed to admit 'in house' consultants to membership on the grounds that these are as free to offer independent and objective advice as the rest of the membership. If the trend towards managerial independence continues – and the indications are that it will – it should bring a new dimension to the organization and control of consultants by blurring the boundaries between employed and self-employed where expertise is in short supply.

The accountancy firms differ from the general consultancy practices in seeking to maintain the traditional divisions in this respect. Ernest Barnes, the Senior UK Partner of Price Waterhouse Associates, is particularly adamant about it. 'As a matter of policy we do not use casual people, or associates, or part timers or anything of that sort,' he says firmly. 'Where we lack expertise, we form an association with another consultancy operation of some quality.' His argument is that it is not possible to guarantee the standards of work of non-employees. 'By going to other consulting groups where we know they have the same sort of standards, we know the firm will stand behind the individual and provide the supervision necessary to make sure that the quality of his job is right.'

Nevertheless, the accountant firms are just as much part of the merging and spawning process which is a strong feature of the consulting business as it strives to exchange and modernize its expertise as are the traditional practices. Even the most conservative of accounting institutions see nothing wrong with the acquisition of ready-made specialist units. Equally they accept that they will shed trained professionals who continue the cycle by setting up specialist units.

The company doctor

Arthur Hallwood, a consultant who gave sole practitioners and small firms a powerful voice within the profession for the first time in the mid-1970s, is one example of an accountant who has made several switches between employed, self-employed, and partner status. Hallwood describes the work he most enjoys as that of being 'a company life saver'. Significantly, he wanted to become a medical doctor after war service as a pilot, but the waiting list was too long and he trained as an accountant instead.

Hallwood is called in, usually by a bank or finance house, to assess if an ailing company is viable, and if it is, to turn it round. This can require quick reactions. On one occasion, he remembers being given only two hours to see people and scrutinize accounts before jumping into a taxi with the solicitors to stop the law courts from issuing a winding up order. The courts gave a stay of two weeks, during which time Hallwood had to work out a plan for the business to be put right. His view was that the management was good technically but that it had neglected to collect its debts and pay its bills: 'They had an awful lot of money there, but they hadn't bothered chasing it,' he says.

One of Hallwood's lifesaving actions in such circumstances is to negotiate with both debtors and creditors but he also attempts to show the management how to do things better in the future. In this particular case, he proceeded to find an investment holding company from among his many City contacts to take over the business. 'It is now doing very well,' he says. 'I see its products all over the place.'

Hallwood, who has been in the profession for almost thirty years, gained his initial training as a consultant with PA whom he joined after having spent the then obligatory couple of years in industry. He added a thorough grounding in work study, production control and manufacturing industry generally to his accountancy qualifications during the eight years he spent with the firm. He left PA in the 1960s, mainly because there was a long wait for promotion and he 'didn't feel he was getting anywhere'; also because he was 'fed up with being shoved around'. After an interim spell as managing director of a loss-making group of companies which was later taken over by a conglomerate, he set up on his own because he was attracted by an organizational assignment, overseas, offered by a former client. After about a year, family commitments led him to seek a greater level of security and he became a partner with a firm of accountants where he continued to work mainly abroad. 'I thoroughly enjoyed the work, but I got desperately tired after about four years of it.'

At the time of writing, he has been operating as a sole practitioner for about twelve years concentrating on work which interests him. 'I'm not usually interested in something unless it is in a real mess,' he says; and he has built up a sufficiently wide reputation for clients to beat a path to his door. He has been asked many times to become a company receiver but has so far refused because he doesn't think he 'would be tough enough'.

In the early 1970s Hallwood became interested in the Institute of Management Consultants and took on the secretaryship and later the chairmanship of the London Branch of the Institute. Here he became aware of the requirements of other small consulting firms in gaining introductions both to each other and to prospective clients. By energetic championship he sparked a series of initiatives, one of which later became the Institute's Professional Register, and which cumulatively may have a profound effect on the development and survival of the profession in years to come.

The consultants' consultant

Human relations is identified by management consultants and

management gurus alike as the key area for the future. This is seen as both the main barrier against and the main force for the changes which are regarded as essential if British industry is to have a meaningful role in tomorrow's markets. The more enlightened companies are preaching the necessity for leadership in areas such as employee involvement, individual motivation and communications. Management consultants, as is to be expected, are well aware of their clients' hopes in this respect. At the same time, they are conscious that much of their present work is concerned with rectifying past mistakes, particularly in the field of incentive and bonus schemes.

George Doris, a principal consultant with The P–E Consulting Group added a study and experience of behavioural science to his professional training as a mining engineer in order to win a better understanding of industrial relations. He tends towards scepticism about the benefits of incentive schemes, believing that although the prospect of higher awards can motivate in the initial 'honeymoon' period, it is difficult to prevent abuse and decay in the longer term.

Having graduated and worked as a colliery under-manager and then in a succession of management jobs with a private engineering firm, Doris joined P–E in 1957. While a newly trained mining engineer he had liked the experience of investigation and reporting and this eventually influenced him to join a consulting firm.

In his years with P–E, Doris has gained firsthand experience of the distortions which resulted from many of the early productivity schemes through advising organizations like Harland and Wolfe, United Glass, Thames Board Mills, the National Coal Board and British Rail: 'I used to see myself as a kind of industrial pathologist,' he recalls.

He underwent experiential learning in behavioural sciences both at the Tavistock Institute in Britain and at the NTL (National Training Laboratory) in the United States while continuing to practise as a consultant and also leading training groups of his own. He found that the three activities reinforced each other, in that knowledge gained from the institutes gave new insight into his consulting relationships with his clients and into his training activities and vice versa. He describes the process as 'very much a personally initiated self-development programme'.

As an example of the type of assignment he finds particularly interesting, Doris cites the case of the British subsidiary of a multinational chemical corporation:

> In 1980, the chief executive of this company sought my help in organising and facilitating a comprehensive 'business review' in which four teams of managers, each headed by a main board director, investigated and reported on the effectiveness of the several divisions. The consultant's task here was to provide training in the processes of investigation; attend meetings and contribute to the development of reports; hold 'a mirror up to the organisation' and push them to handle some sticky issues; and help to make sense of the many useful proposals for organisational and other change that emerged.

In tackling this work Doris found himself using all the experience he had accumulated over the years and says 'an on-going relationship with the company continues, with several assignments to do with organisation and productivity having been completed subsequently'.

The endless argument

Distinctions between the generalist and the specialist management consultant are the subject of endless argument among consultants themselves. Some of the older consultants claim that much confusion could have been avoided if technical advisers, industrial engineers and management engineers had not all been encouraged to use the generic description of 'management consultant', after World War II.

But the flaw with the concept of there being two distinct categories of management consultant, the specialist and the generalist, is that people do not remain in separate, watertight compartments. A specialist can very quickly broaden and develop. Equally, a generalist may choose to concentrate on a particular activity and neglect others. A management consultant has a privileged opportunity for self-development in either direction because of the variety of his work and because he is constantly being exposed to new thinking in his chosen discipline – assuming, of course, that he can survive the pace.

The big British consultancies, like their American counterparts, operate on an 'Up or Out' basis. If after three or four years a consultant does not seem to be making the grade he is encouraged, gently in some cases and less so in others, to move back into industry. Persuasion to move out of consulting does not necessarily carry any suggestion of lack of ability. It is simply that different, and rather special, skills are needed for consultancy: good consultants do not necessarily make good managers and vice versa.

By temperament, all management consultants must be able to operate on a project basis – to become absorbed, complete and then disengage from a problem. They need to identify essential components but retain an eye for the small details which enable them to communicate effectively at all levels within the client organization. They need to become emotionally involved, but retain their objectivity.

Consultants working for the big firms have developed a chameleon quality which enables them to blend with any background. In contrast, those working as independents display a refreshing individuality even though they too have been recruited from the same pool, and in many instances undergone their initial training in one of the traditional 'big four' practices.

The increase in number of independents who now account for about 40 per cent of the Institute of Management Consultants' membership has been one of the remarkable features of the last decade. Some of these were forcibly shaken out of the big firms by the recessionary forces of the early and mid 1970s. Others got fed up with constant travel, irregular hours and disruption to family life. But a third category quit of their own volition, because of frustrated ambition and also because of dissatisfaction with inept implementation of their proposals.

The change has been not only in the quantity of small consultancy practices but also in their quality. Consultants in large firms tend to speak disparagingly about their smaller counterparts. (There is a tendency towards jealousy in all professions, but more so in consulting than in most others.) On the one hand, there is a tendency to write off sole practitioners as semi-retired consultants who prefer a quiet rural life. On the other, there is an assumption that proprietors of small firms oversell themselves and will sooner or later come to financial grief. There is, however, a middle course which has created a new pool of a hundred or more thriving small consultancy businesses run by vigorous and ambitious management consultants.

Consultants in large practices traditionally rely heavily on voluminous reports which, apart from the names on the covers, have few features in content or style to distinguish the work of one firm from a rival. Independents still produce neatly typed reports, but they work much more closely with their clients on a personal basis. One firm of recruiting specialists will provide temporary management as an aid to drawing up a job specification before seeking a candidate. Another, which specializes in investigating overseas markets is very unhappy, according to its proprietor, 'if we come back at the end of a job without some firm enquiries from potential customers and a short-list of importing agents or better still, some actual orders. If you come back with business, they will jolly well have to believe your recommendations and do something about them. We also get involved to the extent that we are very unhappy to carry out a study overseas unless somebody from the client company is working alongside us. They don't have just to believe our reports, they have experienced it for themselves.'

If the independents are not predominantly mercenaries when they first set up on their own, trading conditions during a recession very quickly force them to become so. A tendency for clients to wish to bargain over consultancy fees is a feature of the current cost-cutting environment mentioned by several small firms. 'We very quickly learned to offer a series of price options,' said the proprietor of one firm formed (by an ex-PA consultant) about seven years ago. New methods of remuneration other than fees related to consultant's time and related to the results achieved are constantly being investigated. An acceptable formula has not emerged so far, but the signs are that one soon will. At the time of writing one proprietor is considering a deal under which he would accept half the normal fee rate and expenses on condition that he is also given a percentage share of the new business which results from his activities.

Where does this, then, leave the idealists and the visionaries? This is a question which consultants frequently ask of themselves and to which there is no easy answer. However, most management consultants have an emotional involvement in leaving a business in better shape than they found it. They are temperamentally unsuited to working under conditions of continuous retrenchment. Optimists believe that new leaders will emerge with economic recovery.

10
The Challenge of the Future

Two main thrusts can be perceived in demand for management consultancy services in the 1980s and 1990s. One arises from the drive towards installing more advanced technologies to maintain international competitiveness in industry and commerce. The other is in the education and motivation of people to make maximum use of the new equipment.

Perhaps the most significant development of the 1970s was the growth of computer related consulting. The big practices are being increasingly involved in the use of computers for operations including management information systems, materials management, and production control. Computerized techniques are now established in such areas as marketing, job evaluation, personnel records and financial analysis. Of perhaps more long-term significance has been the rapid growth of software services in the larger traditional consultancies. In at least one major consulting firm, earnings from software services now exceed those arising from pure management consulting. As a result, the profession generally and particularly the large firms are moving away from the classical management consulting of the 1960s to the provision of computer related management services.

Advanced technologies have already swept through large sections of manufacturing. Next on the horizon is automation in offices with the commercial sector including banks, insurance companies, building societies, retailers and travel firms taking the lead.

The planning and design of the new business information systems alone is likely to generate much work for consultants for at least the rest of this decade and probably well into the next.

New competition

Even before the sharp reduction in employment experienced as a result of the 1980–81 slump in manufacturing, British companies were finding it increasingly acceptable to use outside services. The process of dismantling the big industrial conglomerates formed in the 1960s shook out many central 'in house' departments which were then replaced by contracted-out services. Far from reaching saturation, the market for consultancy and related management services in Britain appears to be not only widening but expanding. The arrival of executive search agencies and computer software houses are just two examples of the many new opportunities for consultants which evolved during the 1970s. They demonstrated not only the expansion in the market requirements, but also the speed with which rival organizations can spring up if established management consulting groups fail to adapt to their customers' requirements.

The next decade is likely to bring yet more competition. Smaller and medium-sized practitioners will encounter new rivals among specialist outsiders whose ranks will be augmented by experts shaken out of industry and government by the slump. Big practices will meet steeper opposition at home from the accounting-based groups, whose management consulting subsidiaries are superbly placed for development in financial services and office automation –two of the sectors most strongly tipped for growth.

Along with the increase in small firms and sole practitioners, the increase in the management consulting subsidiaries of the accountancy groups has been one of the outstanding features of the last decade. Computers which were first applied to company finance departments gave them a big boost, although, with hindsight, accountants as well as general management consultants blame themselves for not paying sufficient attention to computers in the 1960s.

Businesses relate to each other through their finance departments, through cheques and invoices exchanged between customer and supplier. Finance departments also form a link between business and Government and via the payroll between employer and employee. Any change of tax requirements, payroll or invoicing procedures of one organization is therefore likely to be first felt in the finance department of another.

Some accountancy firms acquired management consultancy practices to meet the new demands, others developed their own departments. By the middle 1960s, accountancy firms were offering a range of consultancy services which in addition to covering management accounting took in production and marketing – areas which had previously been considered almost the exclusive province of the traditional 'big four'.

The inflationary 1970s were kinder to the accountancy practices than to general management consultants. There were new demands for financial services of all kinds ranging from decimalization to the introduction of Value Added Tax, apart from the wider pressures of managing cash flows and investments.

Several factors continue to work to the advantage of the accounting-based practices and will do so for the foreseeable future. The prime one is, of course, continuity of income arising from audit work. Accounting groups do not always care to admit to using it, but there is wide scope for cross-subsidy of expertise and facilities within the professional divisions of a group. This, in turn, provides a more secure operating base from which to breed new developments. There are also advantages in the much older traditions and experience which accountants have had in the organization and control of professional employees.

The 1980s have brought the accountants more new work stemming from company closures, liquidations and bankruptcy. They are equally well-placed to assist with management buy-outs, and the starting up of new firms as economic conditions improve. Executives in the traditional 'big four' look on enviously as accounting groups move further into the 'classical' management consulting arena. At the time of writing Price Waterhouse is carrying out a basic organizational study into British Airways involving about a dozen consultants scrutinizing fields as varied as the airline's ticket pricing strategies and its redundancy policy as well as its approach to price competition across the North Atlantic routes.

The rigorously observed quality controls and monitoring systems which the accountancy firms have applied to their consultancy operations as well as to their audit work have paid off handsomely in bringing in new customers. The accountancy groups seem set fair to provide the biggest challenge in the home market to the traditional consultancy practices in the next decade. Abroad, there is new competition not only from American opponents but also from local consulting groups, an increasing number of which will be staffed by ex-employees.

Despite the overall expansion, therefore, the effect of increased competition may mean that the traditional consulting firms can reap few of the benefits, unless they themselves can change their own attitudes and work practices. In particular, tomorrow's consultants will no longer be able to afford ambivalence about whether or not they are in business. They will have to devote the same approach to pricing and promoting their own products as they recommend to their clients.

More professional clients

In addition to operating in a much more competitive market, tomorrow's management consultants will have to adjust to changes within their client organizations. Managers generally have become markedly better educated and more articulate; and above all, they have a keener eye for value for money than they had a decade ago. They are also able to do for themselves much of the work which was formerly carried out by management consultants. The trend is for assignments to be shorter and more precise, lasting for a matter of days or weeks rather than months (or even, in some cases, years).

Since consultants' fees are related to the time they spend on the job the trend towards shorter assignments has obvious implications for the economics of the profession. Most organizations already operate a tiered charging structure. A consultant engaged on overall strategic planning for a business at, say, about £2,000 per week (1982 prices) may cost three times the rate of a consultant operating on a production planning project. On the other hand, strategic and high level consulting assignments are generally the shortest. 'You can go into a company, get a feel of it, its environment, its competition, its facilities on the shop floor, its organization – the threats, the opportunities, the strengths and the weaknesses. You can then give a view to the Board as to what could be done for the future – all in about three weeks,' explained Len Weaver of P–E. However the bulk of general consultancy work is in less rarefied strata and is carried out in areas like production and inventory control, energy and material utilization or operator training which require different and more readily obtained skills from consultants and therefore cost less.

The trend towards even wider differentials in consultancy charges is likely to be accelerated by several factors. Client organizations have had to become leaner in the last few years, partly as a result of work carried out by earlier generations of consultants, and partly in response to economic stringencies. They will no longer have as much available labour capacity to work with consultants. More efficient programmed learning systems and measurement tools will take over some of the supporting work but there will also be a need for larger numbers of researchers, auditors, computer programmers and other staff of more junior grades than consultant to be supplied externally for a limited time and at cheaper rates.

At the other end of the cost spectrum is the increase in the degree of specialization required from consultants. Production and inventory control systems have been changed out of all recognition by computer developments and highly sophisticated software packages. Advances in microcomputers, word processors, and telecommunications are working their way through administration areas. Training, which was once a foundation of basic consultancy operations, is now a highly specialist area.

Separate identities

Although the debate still rumbles on whenever consultants meet and talk together, it seems clear that there will be little room in tomorrow's business environment for practices which are jacks of all trades, if they are masters of none. Leaders of the traditional big groups are well aware of the challenges which are facing them and are making strenuous efforts to adjust. At PA for instance, general consulting work, which takes in everything from production and inventory control through energy and material utilization, now accounts for just under 50 per cent of the total business and is only one of five functional areas. The remainder comes from personnel services; computers; telecommunications; and management training. PA is expanding its network of Patscentre new product development laboratories as well as Pactel, its specialist consultancy in computing, telecommunications, and office automation.

Inbucon has recently acquired a technology transfer and licensing subsidiary in order to identify internationally made advances on behalf of its British clients. More than 25 per cent of The P–E Consulting Group's turnover comes from oil and energy-related industrial clients; and well over half its assignments have a significant computer element. Urwick Orr, smallest of the traditional 'big four', has a well developed presence in the computer area with Urwick Dynamics.

While the views and perspectives of the senior executives in the major firms naturally vary, there is a general belief that increasing specialization will be the order of the day for the 1980s. Significant differences are already apparent between them in the range and nature of services provided. Ten years ago, a client might well have invited competitive quotes from all of the 'big four' but this is unlikely to happen today.

Companies requiring assistance with computerized management accounting systems are likely to single out one of the accounting firms rather than the major management consultancies, whereas those seeking help with new product development are likely to turn to PA. Consultant users requiring assistance with manufacturing systems and technology would very likely include P–E in the list of consultants invited to tender. Inbucon have a similar reputation in the field of industrial relations; and Urwick Orr, in the area of office automation.

The differences between the major consulting firms are likely to widen during the coming decade. Competitive and economic pressures will mean that major consulting firms will have to be much more selective about areas of development and much more positive about dispensing with those services for which there is a declining demand. The degree of investment and the nature of the specialist development in each firm will clearly vary. As a result, competition between the major firms will reduce and the likelihood of them collaborating in quoting for major assignments – particularly those overseas – will increase.

People problems

Much less activity is visible in the 'people', 'human relations', or behavioural science front identified by the consultancy leaders as another main area for future development. One reason is that the traditional consultancies already have strong roots in human relations. Another is, quite simply, absence of heavy demand from clients.

The Employment Protection Act of 1975 increased consultants' activities in the personnel field. Management Consultants Association figures show that, at 24 per cent, members' activities in personnel management and selection were approximately double the proportion recorded ten years earlier. The Bullock Committee's report published in January 1977 and the Government White Paper in the same year generated some interest and considerable controversy amongst employers over the question of industrial democracy and worker participation.

Controls on pay increased interest in productivity schemes and fringe benefits.

The traditional theory was that an increase in demand for consultancy skills in negotiation, introduction and training would accompany the installation of the new electronic equipment and the new systems and procedures associated with it. There are few signs, as yet, of any such increase. Instead, the indications are that high unemployment, the recession, and the waning of trade union influence are tempting companies to bypass or at least speed up many of the stages in the labour relations side of the installation processes. It remains to be seen whether what trade union leaders describe as the 'born again' managements of today are repeating old mistakes or whether the principles of consultation learned with such difficulty during the last decade will be applied in the next.

The Japanese-inspired idea of 'Quality Circles' has been the one development in the behavioural science area which has sparked management interest, so far, in the 1980s. Nancy Foy, a manager with Standard Telephones and Cables and an author, has described how these developed at STC and indicates some of the difficulties in getting them to operate effectively:

> When STC started quality circles we found many managers wanted to know how much money would be saved or how much productivity would increase. I finally coined a 'rule' to cope with this instinct: 'Management Mustn't Measure'. The benefits of the quality circles were qualitative, not quantitative.
>
> We wanted better products, and better working conditions, and better morale, and more enthusiasm, and more ideas and ultimately an improvement in the quality of working life as well as the quality of the products. An emphasis on counting would have been counter-productive. If a quality circle suggestion saved £50,000 then would the

next one be less good because it only saved £5?

The approach that worked was to give the quality circles the tools they needed to measure for themselves the things they wanted to measure. One group wanted a machine moved in a way that would cost £5,000. They made a representation to a factory manager, who asked them to estimate how the expense would be justified. They did this – conservatively, as it turned out – and the manager was able to approve the change, on the same rational grounds as any change proposed by a management team. But the real payoff was not just in the savings they predicted (the new layout saved time every time runs were changed) but in the involvement and commitment of the members of that group.

[*The Guardian*, 8 January 1982]

Management consultants are well aware of the opportunities for their services in developments such as Quality Circles. Any of the big consultancies would be delighted to explain the principles behind them to their clients. However, they are also aware that relatively few companies have direct experience of introducing them and many managers are sceptical of what some regard as yet another fashionable technique which may soon disappear. But given the guarded acceptance by the Trades Union Congress, Quality Circles are seen as one method of opening up much needed channels of direct internal communication between employer and employee.

Management consultants are equally aware of the need identified by some management leaders for the elimination of status symbols and privileges in areas such as canteens, cars, holidays, hours worked, pensions, sickness benefits and job security. But again, they are waiting for an invitation from their clients before offering their services to resolve the difficulties associated with the removal of such 'perks'.

The emphasis in the 1970s was on increasing productivity through the elimination of jobs. Management consultants have had long experience in identifying unnecessary labour and devising ways of removing it right the way through organizations from factory floor to boards of directors. With unemployment totals touching the previously unthinkable 3 million mark there will be much more stress on job creation in the 1980s.

British management consultants have carried out extensive work on this front abroad in developing countries. Brian Woodhead, the 1982 President of the Institute of Management Consultants, cites the example of a construction project which his own company has been carrying out for the World Bank. It involves the use of labour rather than plant to construct roads in a country which is desperately short of jobs.

Picks and shovels are provided rather than excavators or bulldozers. Work is carried out by battalions of people housed in special camps and recruited from local villages. As the road moves along, so more are recruited. The reason for using such old-fashioned methods, apart from the fact that it creates jobs, is that such roads are created in inaccessible places where it would be difficult to provide and maintain plant and in areas where, for reasons of political instability, it may be unwise to invest a lot of capital. The consultant operates as the administrator and accountant working alongside the civil engineer back at an administrative headquarters, which worries about paying people, stock control and organizing supplies of local materials.

The independents' view

Woodhead feels quite strongly that the days of the large scale consultancy practice are over except as consortia of wide ranges of specialists. He thinks that too much consultancy has been pre-packaged in the past, and is a firm believer in the individual tailor-made solution. Woodhead is a typical example of a proprietor of one of the newer generation of small consultancy firms. Trained by PA, he left in 1974 to form his own company. Initially his idea was to act as a broker to negotiate assignments and put clients in touch with appropriate consultancy practices. Latterly, however, after some bad experiences using established consultancy firms, he has moved into the control and supervision of assignments using self-employed 'associates' working under his company's banner hiring specialists for specific tasks. From this, other services developed including temporary management, career development counselling, and business opportunities – i.e. providing assistance with mergers and acquisitions or by expanding a company's trading base. A recent diversification has been into industrial advertising.

The most complex management consulting job which the company has carried out so far involved a rationalization exercise for a nationalized industry when four consultants looked at the scope for combining on one site a number of operations previously carried out in a variety of areas. 'We looked at everything from marketing to office accommodation including the protection of the individual components' identity through the use of separate telephone lines,' commented Woodhead.

Another leader in the small firms consultancy arena is Roland Orr, the 1982 chairman of the Sole Practitioners and Small Firms Group of the London Region of the Institute of Management Consultants and a member of the Institute's Council. Orr believes that the small firms will mostly stay small. Only a tiny minority of the small practices will expand above five principals. The main expansion will be through the use of 'associates' or self-employed consultants.

One new development is a group of about 60 independent consultants who, for marketing reasons, are attempting to set up a loose network. The Richmond Group is based mainly in Southeast England and once it gets started will consist entirely of members of the Institute of Management Consultants.

The general feeling among the Institute of Management Consultants' committee which Orr chairs is that most sole practitioners will have to specialize and become the leaders of innovation in their own areas if they are to become successful. Likely areas include the 'people' disciplines (executive search and selection, industrial relations, marketing, personnel, training, and management development) and the smaller business systems concerned with administration and planning. The small firms and sole practitioners' group did not think its members could compete effectively with their larger counterparts on large scale data processing systems assignments, but they would like a larger share of public sector consultancy contracts.

Innovators or followers

The small management consultancy practices are riding on the crest of general support for small businesses which are a strong feature of the 1980s as part of the overall drive to regenerate industry. Given powerful Government support and patronage from some prestigious large firms, the 'small is beautiful' slogan may become a significant business reality of the next decade.

Like their larger counterparts, however, the small consultancy firms react to rather than initiate changes. Their lower overheads and small staffs enable them to react quicker and more flexibly to user requirements, but they too tend to be followers rather than innovators. Today's new thinking stems mainly from the business schools and those quasi-governmental institutions which have survived purges on public expenditure. Tomorrow's consulting leaders may stem from management's own ranks.

There are large numbers of itinerant executives in circulation within the bigger corporations who have become self-taught management consultants. Some of these will gravitate towards the big practices once demand for their particular skills increases. Others may develop independently initially as advisers to their former employers but gradually building up an external clientele. Training executives are one likely source of recruits to the future ranks of management consultants. Another is personnel managers, whose numbers have more than trebled since the 1960s. There are, however, wide varieties of specialist executives who have been shaken loose from their niches by the recession waiting for new openings.

Bending old rules

The traditional consultancy firms have already widened their previously rigid recruiting policies. New entrants are no longer confined to young men in their late twenties or early thirties, nor are they expected to make a lifetime career of consulting. Tomorrow's management consultants can expect to move much more easily into industry and back again. Attitudes towards the use of 'associates' or subcontractors have already relaxed considerably.

'Going back ten or fifteen years, we didn't dream of using associates,' says Ken Hampton, the managing director of PA. 'We are using them more now, partly because it enables us to have a specialist who might not have a full-time role when the assignment demands and partly because it enables us to have a more stable permanent staff in a fluctuating economy.'

The rest of the big consulting firms have equally adopted a similar, more flexible attitude to the acquisition of expertise. Pooling of experts in this way could result in greater cross-transference between the consulting firms. Since it is rare for a consultant trained and employed by one practice to work for another, the only opportunity for most consultants to meet colleagues in rival practices has been through professional institutions. The isolation in which consultants work and the jealousy with which they have historically guarded their individual experience has hindered the development of the overall 'body of knowledge' of the profession.

By breaking down the traditional barriers between the firms, the more fluid working environments of the 1980s may help the development of unique features by which consultant firms can distinguish themselves from their competitors. These unique features might be in one or another management technique or a corner in a particular industry, a special consulting approach, or method of operating.

Pooling expertise

With economic recovery and an increase in demand for consultancy work, some of the individuals and groups, many of which will be ex-employees who are at present working on an 'associate' basis, may become reabsorbed back into the large companies. After seasoning and experience in a different school they could be candidates for leadership of the firms.

The large consulting firms are well aware of the difficulties in the current environment of retaining and motivating able and ambitious consultants. The development of potential new managers is one reason why The P–E Consulting Group, for instance, is considering replacing a single conglomerate organizational structure with a holding company and several subsidiary businesses. 'Each of these would be very different in that they would be recruiting their own personnel, perhaps at different salary levels, terms and conditions and they would provide rather different services to separate markets,' explains Len Weaver, the managing director. 'The overlap between these businesses would be limited because they would all offer specialized services and use different methods of marketing.'

Streamlining

Weaver emphasises the implications of specialization. 'The range of services provided by the large companies will be gradually reduced in order to accommodate greater levels of specialization. Achievement of greater specialization and sophistication in areas such as computer aided engineering, information technology, robotics and even management training requires increasingly greater investment in specialist staff, personnel development and the associated technology. It is therefore essential to be selective now in making decisions about the services one will be offering in two or three years.'

Increasing demand for specialization has led to PA forming industry sector groups covering, for instance, the oil and gas or financial services areas and which operate internationally. Specialization is likely to cause it to pay more attention to the functional strand rather than the geographical aspect of its activities in the future although these will complement rather than replace the firm's existing comprehensive network of sixty-five overseas offices which also provide career development opportunities for consultants.

The traditional firms are seen as continuing to provide an important training ground for new recruits to the profession, but one which will gradually diminish as the effects of the recruitment bulge of the middle and late 1960s and the retrenchment of the early and middle 1970s work their way through. The accountancy groups, which were better able to keep up their intake of newcomers in the 1970s, will increase in importance. But tomorrow's management consultants of distinction may stem from some new and unexpected source. They may come from some of the scientists employed at present by the specialist software houses or from entrepreneurial businessmen who have learnt from the experience of running a company and wish to pass on their knowledge to others.

A perceptible increase in the willingness of British companies to seek outside advice is a feature of the current business environment compared with that of a decade ago.

At the same time, the emphasis (as also in management education and industrial training) is on self-development and on evolution from within an organization rather than on looking for answers from outside. In order to sow new ideas in a self-learning climate, a single consultant needs to spend only a few hours with a handful of employees and then make periodic checks on progress. This is consistent with the Urwick philosophy that 'The only work that is really worth doing as a consultant is that which educates –which teaches clients and their staff to manage better for themselves,' but it provides a slender base from which to run a consultancy business based on fees.

According to one school of thought, the non-executive director may take over some of the strategic functions previously provided by management consultants. It is interesting to note that many sole practitioners hold several such appointments, although companies are said to be showing an increasing preference for directors who have had a background in management rather than consultancy for such appointments. Another view is that, if used properly, a non-executive director becomes too involved with the company concerned to take an objective stand and any attempt to do so merely adds to the internal factions which can hinder rather than facilitate the introduction of change.

There are boundless opportunities in the changes which are on the business horizon if the current intake of consultants can survive in an environment where their status as experts is no longer taken for granted and if they can also develop the breadth which was so prized by their predecessors. The explosion in information technology which is just around the corner will bring the facilities for total electronic communication to the end of each manager's desk. If he chooses to use it in this way it will not only enormously increase his own department's ability to store, retrieve, and process data, but can also give him instant access to the work of his counterparts in other divisions. This, in turn, can increase awareness of the necessity for different components of a business to interlock as a whole.

The first priority must be to re-establish a stable productive base. Only then will it be possible to resume the wider debate about the relationship between jobs and reward, and work and leisure, on which society's long-term future depends. Management consultants are actively involved in the first part of this process. It would be a tragedy if their present business preoccupations prevented them from contributing to the second.

Further Reading

Currie, R. M., *Work Study* (London: British Institute of Management, 1959).

Flanders, A. *The Fawley Productivity Agreements* (London: Faber, 1964).

Glyn, A. and Harrison, J. *The British Economic Disaster* (Pluto Press, 1980).

Humble, J. W. *Management by Objectives in Action* (McGraw-Hill, 1970).

Hyman, S. *An Introduction to Management Consultancy* (London: Heinemann, 1961).

Kubr, M. ed. *Management Consulting — A Guide to the Profession* (Geneva: ILO).

Margerison, C. Influencing Organisational Change (London: Institute of Personnel Management, 1978).

Marks, W. *Politics and Personnel Management — An Outline History* (London: Institute of Personnel Management, 1978).

Shaw, A. G. *An Introduction to the Theory and Application of Motion Study* (Harlequin Press, 1953).

Shaw, A. G. *The Purpose & Practice of Motion Study* (Columbine Press).

Shay, P. *How to Get the Best Results from Management Consultants* (American Association of Consulting Management Engineers, 1974).

Tatham, L. *The Efficiency Experts — An Impartial Survey of Management Consultancy* (Business Publications, 1964).

Townsend, R. *Up the Organization* (London: Michael Joseph, 1970).

Whitehead, H. *The Administration of Marketing and Selling* (London: Pitman, 1937).

Modernisation in the Cotton Spinning Industry — A Report on Labour Redeployment in the Musgrage Mill Cardroom Bolton (The Labour Department of the Cotton Board: March 1948).

Report by the Bolton Committee on Small Firms (HMSO, November 1971).

The Manpower Implications of Micro-Electronic Technology. (A report by Jonathan Sleigh, Brian Boatwright, Peter Irwin, Roger Stanyon. Department of Employment/HMSO, 1979).

Index